ALL OUR YESTERDAYS

Doing Pana in the 1940s

ALL OUR YESTERDAYS

DECLAN HASSETT

MERCIER PRESS

IRISH AMERICAN BOOK COMPANY (IABC)
Boulder, Colorado

MERCIER PRESS
PO Box 5, 5 French Church Street, Cork
16 Hume Street, Dublin 2

Trade enquiries to CMD DISTRIBUTION,
55a Spruce Avenue, Stillorgan Industrial Park, Blackrock, Dublin

Published in the US and Canada by the
IRISH AMERICAN BOOK COMPANY
6309 Monarch Park Place, Niwot, Colorado, 80503
Tel: (303) 652 2710, (800) 452-7115
Fax: (303) 652 2689, (800) 401-9705

© Declan Hassett, 1998

ISBN 185635 232 3

10 9 8 7 6 5 4 3 2 1

TO ANNE

Cover photograph: Prayerful procession in 1949, from *The Examiner's Picture That Again*

Printed in Ireland by Colour Books Ltd.

CONTENTS

JUMBLE OF MEMORIES
IN A
CARDBOARD BOX

There is a large cardboard box which has found a permanent home on top of a wardrobe. Now, in my young days, God it only feels like yesterday, my mother's Sunday-best hat, or a valued Christening robe, or Confirmation dress, would have been found there. This box contains a lifetime of photographs; the only images of those lost years lie stacked, waiting as it were, for a proper setting in a family album which will be bought – any day now.

Every time a photograph comes back from the developers, the place and date should be written on the back. I'm surrounded with prints taken on occasions which have long been forgotten and cannot be placed in their proper context. There is the day at the beach, but, what beach, and, who is the child on the fringe on that half-forgotten sunlit day?

There are joys too in this jumble of the past. Finding the photo you thought you had lost and there it is, stuck on the back of another. Its finding releases a succession of fond memories about a day at the sea when a gentle swell belied the fact that we were miles out from the land. It prompts other thoughts too. I don't know if you are prone to sea-sickness but a couple of swells (sounds like a line from a song!) and I'm a whiter shade of pale (another song!) in fact, a decidedly green in the gills type.

One lovely Sunday morning, sandwiches and flasks were packed and the plan was a day's fishing. It was important to me as a prospective father-in-law needed to be impressed with my seamanship. It was not to be. We reached the fishing grounds and you can guess the rest but I'll tell you anyway. I was fine once I kept my eye on the land, but every time I looked down the bottom of the boat came up to meet me. I must be one of the few sailors in the brave history of the sea who had to be dropped off at the nearest headland. When I regained my equilibrium I returned to base through the fields. My arrival back at the pier, by the land route, was a talking point in the village of Guileen for some days.

Didn't know I still had it but I came across the school confirmation photograph. We were marched down from the school, looking like a showband in our blazers and long white pants, school caps perched on heads. We were soldiers of God and must have been a joy to our mothers.

Of course, the really old photographs are best. They recall faces and times which mean so much now to those who may not even have been around at the time. There, in your hands, are another generation at work and play. No doubt they thought too that the good days would never slip by, but they do and all that is left of a wonderful life is a fading photograph lying in an old cardboard box.

Confirmation day at Peter and Paul's

FORBIDDEN FRUITS

My grandfather's proudest possession was a fine orchard and he spent his last years guarding it from his vantage points of either a seat under the lean-to, or, sitting in a chair, looking out through a large window in the back-door which, when I think of it, never actually opened.

He was a grand old gentleman about whom almost everyone, who knew him, would to this day, speak well. To me, still in short pants and up to every prank, he appeared a stern authoritarian (I did not know the word then) figure, whose bearded countenance, peering out through the glass, spelt trouble ahead.

I could never quite understand why he would become so upset just because the cousin and myself would shake a few branches and litter the ground underneath with windfalls. One tap on the glass with his cane and it was a scamper down the tree, and, through the bordering hedge, hiding there until the coast was clear. It was important then that there would be no raid for a few days after that, as he'd man the look-out from dawn to dusk, at least until he was sure I was in bed.

I do not know to this day if he ever actually complained to our parents but I was cute enough to leave well alone when nothing was said. What I came to admire in the man afterwards was that when we'd first meet after the incident, he'd make no reference to it, but put his large arms around me and tell me how quickly I was growing up. I suppose for the man quickly was not really quick enough, but he never let on. My abiding memory was having to give a kiss goodbye after visits; I hated the feel of the grey beard and I think he knew that, so that might have been his revenge for all the upset I caused him.

In that orchard there was quite the most magical chicken house which would, when the birds had gone, serve as a store-house for the apples and the few pears which came from the trees which he had growing against a south-facing wall.

There was a large window to the front of the wooden structure but this had been nailed shut and chicken wire placed over the glass. When the door was padlocked, entrance could only be through a small opening which had a lift-up, drop-down hatch, just the size for the Rhode Island Reds and the White Leghorns to slip in and out. The chickens were later moved to a larger area in the garden so that first autumn, the apples were placed in the hut, layer on layer in the old orange boxes of no further use in the aunt's shop.

No wonder the poor man's hair was snow white. Yes, you've guessed it, we found we could wriggle in and out just like the chickens. Lord, there was no camp, no secret hideaway which ever compared with that hut under the apple trees. We'd eat only the best of the fruit, needless to mention, and then, joy of joys, there'd be a packet of five Woodbines to be smoked with sinful pleasure.

The memory is a fierce trickster and I never remember becoming very ill in the process but I have been told that there was one occasion when I was as sick as a dog when they came to bring me home. Like the lobster in the pot I had climbed in but was in no state to even crawl out. Adults are very wise. They took one look at me and decided that I would suffer that night for those stolen hours in the hen-house.

I suppose the fact that those were forbidden fruits to a young boy made them that much more sweet.

COMIC CAPERS

It's rummage time. You know what I mean. The mist clings to everything, pervasive and depressing. But he's your only man for opening a conversation ... the weather.

We rummage when there is nothing else to do. We turn things over just to fill time as the overcoat hangs sodden in the hall and the last umbrella has turned itself inside out and lies rejected in the yard waiting for bin morning.

My rummage turned up an old *Beano* comic. Some of the characters are as real to me now as they were then, when I'd race down the Western Road from Pres primary to collect my weekly order of the *Beano, Dandy* and *Radio Fun*. That order would change with the natural gravitas of years to *The Champion* and *Hotspur.*

I find it hard to capture exactly what they meant to a lad in the 1940s and 1950s but I can clearly recall the anticipation of their arrival in the shop each week. There was not the range of magazines that there is now, so the comics would have pride of place, usually on the counter, and we'd line up feeling fierce important that our order would be held for us even if we were all school cap and little else.

Upstairs in the bus, we'd skim through the pages of each edition, not looking at the final picture sequence of each story so that we could savour how our heroes and heroines fared when we got home. I can recall enjoying Lord Snooty and his pals with Snitch and Snatch. Then there was Desperate Dan and later on Dennis the Menace and, or course, Korky the Kat. I think Billy Bunter appeared in *The Champion* and I remember how there was much more reading in this with its attractive blue print.

Later too there was the influence of Radio Luxembourg as Dan Dare would be the hero in the glossy, almost broadsheet size *Eagle* comic. I loved *Radio Fun* and *Film Fun* and, strangely, I can only recall two of the characters from these, Jimmy Jewel and Ben Warris (I think!), who were comedians with their own show on BBC Light.

I do not know if Dick Barton ever got into comics but he was compulsive listening every night for fifteen minutes. He got into trouble every evening about seven and, believe it or not, he'd be free by 6.45 the following night. That's the beauty of fiction, it is much more exciting than real life. Anyway, we thought Dick Barton was real life and schooldays were fiction.

Each week, there was the great comic swap. I had the advantage here because an uncle in America or, rather, his American-born wife, would sEndus packages of *Dell* comics. *Superman* and *Davy Crockett* would figure in these and I know that *Dagwood* and *Blondie* were favourites too.

You must remember there was no television, so all our imagery came from the artistry of the men in Thompson House in Scotland and Dell Publishing in America. I knew every twist and flight of Superman and I fell in love with Lois Lane decades before Clark Kent changed his shirt in a phone box on the big screen and on video in our living-rooms.

We cannot under-estimate the educational role played by these comics in our young lives. They opened our imaginations and introduced us to a world of adventure and romance, all for a few old pence. We could go flying over the skyscrapers of New York and we knew the shape of the Empire State Building. All in all, we were much travelled young fellows as we tamed the Commanches and rode into the sunset.

LITTLE SIGNS OF THINGS TO COME

'Holly Bough, Holly Bough', rang out along damp city streets and I knew Christmas was on its way. Funny how certain events trigger off the same responses each year. I suppose this becomes more understandable as each year passes. So much is changing, we tend to hang on to those things which remind us of our less frenetic past.

This was the time of the year when we'd break out of school on the bell and tear down to Pana (Patrick Street to the visitor) as the window displays of the autumn would be replaced by great pyramids of toys beckoning behind great windows.

Our hot breaths would fog the glass and annoy the man or woman who would be setting the whole thing up. Other shops would place a great sheet of brown paper on the windows before the grand unveiling in late November. Then paradise would beckon a lad with only a few pence in his pocket but total faith in Santa on Christmas Eve night. We never doubted that we would have that Meccano set, or that toy set of farm animals, with its little fences and chickens which remained in the perpetual state of picking up something from the ground.

When I think about it, we must have been the scourge of every shop assistant as we moved around anything that was in our reach, always considering that our sense of display was better. I should point out that this was one of the few advantages of attending a city based school, this street-wise freedom, when our pals, who went to school in the suburbs, would have to get permission to go to town on the bus. All our visits into the toy dens around the town were completed in a relatively short time, so that parents would consider we had just missed the bus and were waiting for the next.

I had a particular favourite around that time. They were the high counters in Woolworths in Patrick Street. Each of those counters had little glass sections which contained different types of toys and the price was clipped

Window to wonderland

on to the rear glass panel. I would spend a whole half hour just wandering from one counter to the other never buying anything, but keeping up to date with all the latest additions to the stock. I would have made a great salesman with such a background.

There were other signs of things to come too. The carol singers who would move from house to house on the week nights before Christmas. At first the voices from a distance, and then the sound would gather as they moved towards each house which would have its own mini-recital before they'd move on into the night. Simple joys, but then they were simpler times.

I suppose we all remember to this day that day, usually a Saturday, when the parents would take us on that special trip to town before Christmas. We never thought of it then, that more than likely our dads would have received something extra in their pay-packets and the visit to town, Santa and a little meal, were by way of a treat. It was a case of hard-earned money being spent on a luxury, a little indulgence for the time that was in it.

Have you ever noticed how the memory can blank out completely whole periods of the past, but little things, like holding your mum or dad's hand in a busy street, or looking up at a particularly frosty sky, can be on total recall many many years later? Was it the impression those moments made, or random tricks of the mind?

There is too that point when Christmas hits you. It may vary for each individual, but, there is no denying that it does creep up, quiet like, and then, from here to there, it's no time at all ... at all.

Interesting then to think about those things which switch you on to Christmas. It could in times past be the mother baking the cake in the kitchen and that sweet aroma which is associated more with this time of the year than any other. There are those who recall the plum-pudding hanging in the pantry, wrapped in muslin cloth; did those puddings ever have an equal in taste, then or ever?

At home, we were fierce entirely for the boiled cakes. Great cutting in them, my mother would say, but they never did last very long. Many mouths were waiting. I loved those thick slices covered in butter, accompanied by a large glass of milk. Your only man for a growing boy.

The *Cork Examiner* would carry news about the up-coming pantos at the old Opera House, Father Matthew, AOH and Father O'Leary Halls, or, in my time, all eyes would be on Coachford where Father Buckley's productions attracted packed houses for their quite stunning staging.

The real buzz for those pantos came on St Stephen's Day when, with parents in tow, we'd head for town in the double-decker bus, a treat in itself, and queue up for the matinee performance. I can still recall overcoming my fear of heights climbing the cast-iron staircase outside the Opera House building. With a sweaty palm locked safely in Dad's large hand, I'd make it to the top and would only open my eyes when I was safely inside 'the Gods'. For those readers who may not have lived, the 'Gods' would be the highest part of the house where a youngster could gaze in silent wonder at the sumptuous auditorium, with those ornate boxes guiding the eyes to the curtain.

The moments before the opening of that curtain, just as the house lights went down, are engraved on my mind. This was anticipation at its most exquisite. Of course it was, as theatre should be, all about magic, illusion and the sense that we had been transported to another world. There, schoolbooks and toothaches did not exist, and here, for a fertile mind, was the reality of life where in a puff of smoke the witch would be transformed into a mouse, and a kiss would always awaken a sleeping princess. Everybody would live happily ever after and that comforting thought would warm us in the cold streets outside after the show. If we were very good, we'd be treated to high tea in a grown-ups' cafe.

The whole afternoon was such a joy that there would be no sleep for hours and hours that night. It would be nice to think that pantos have the same effect on the present generation of children.

TINSEL EXPECTANCY

The man sat on the shopping centre seat and observed the cavalcade. Nearby sat a young lad, waiting for his mum to come out of the shop across the way. Man and boy did not speak to each other, they were wrapped in their own thoughts.

The man was thinking about other times when he would have been about the same age as the lad on the seat, full of the tinsel expectancy of the season; he was again in the big city for the first time with his father who had snatched a few hours off from work to bring his son to see the shops and the lights.

The man could still, without any effort, feel the frost-nip on his nose and cheeks. He held his father's hand as they waded along the footpath, stopping at each window.

It seemed strange now but many of the shops then, even the big ones, had complete cribs scenes displayed, something which would be rare now. They would visit every Santa but he remembered that he told his father that he wanted just one parcel, for a shilling.

God! they were magic to a child. The wrapping paper was delicate pink or blue and Santa had a kind of sentry-box near the top of the stairs in the large shop.

On counters nearby whole farm sets would be laid out, complete with out-houses and fields. Further on, lead toy soldiers lined up against little wheeled guns which, when parents were not looking, could fire matches at the enemy.

One set of six mounted cavalry, black horses, soldiers, with great plumed head-dresses, sword at the shoulder, stayed in the memory-bank long after those same soldiers made their re-appearance in the half-light of a Christmas morning, struggling up the foothills of the patterned bedspread.

The young lad, at the other end of the shopping centre seat, stole a glance at the man and wondered how anyone could look so sad at Christmas time.

The boy had just posted his letter to Santa in the North Pole and made it fairly clear to the great man that one of those computers being advertised on television would do very nicely. He felt he had sealed the bargain by pointing out that dad could, with some help from his son, use the computer too, to do his household accounts.

Dads were easy to get round when you knew how to handle them. Now mothers were a different proposition; they were not as easily led and his mum had pointed out that morning that Santa could decide that a computer was really beyond the means of the lad's family. Santa and mothers were known to join forces like that.

The carol singers moved by the two on the seat and the man was reminded of other voices ringing from house to house, lanterns flicking light along dark roads, voices growing louder as the knock came to the door ... a penny for the poor.

The young lad thought he saw tears trickle down the face of the man but it must have been all the lights playing tricks as surely nobody could be unhappy at this time of the year.

Mum came out of the shop opposite and took the lad in hand, heading for a promised treat in the coffee shop nearby. The man was alone, hardly noticing the little lad's departure. He was thinking of an evening before Christmas, many years ago, when his father had brought him for high tea to the little cafe on the corner. He knew the place must have been posh because they had linen tablecloths.

The centre was emptying so the man got up and slipped out into the cold night air, pulling his coat collar up around his ears and tugging his cap down to meet it. Shoppers' voices carried from car to car in the park as he headed in the direction of the hostel where he was sure of a supper and warm bed.

It was a hard time to be alone.

CHRISTMAS DAY

There is no dawn as welcome as that of Christmas morn. There is that sense of anticipatory calm and stillness, that inner feeling that all is right with the world if only for a day.

For children there is a more material sense of well-being as little eyes open and tiny hands grapple with ruffled quilts, seeking treasures (formed-grey) at the end of beds. There is the rip and tear of crinkly paper as little minds ponder how Santa could ever get round to gift-wrap every single parcel received. Then there is the muster of troops on the landings and the obligatory cavalry charge to parents' rooms, who, God bless their collective hearts, never fail to be surprised at the generosity of Santa Claus.

I can never recall an unhappy Christmas Day. First it was off to Mass with Dad doffing his hat to all who passed by and Mum, ever smiling, making sure we did not lag too far behind. We did not go in for all this saluting, so we children single-filed behind the big man and let him do the pleasantries. He did so to the manner born as through the year he had a word for everyone and took everyone on trust. Not an easy act to follow.

If Santa's parcels had not been found in the bedroom, we would have to hold our breath, honour the Lord and tear home on foot. We'd line up outside the sitting-room door and wait for the signal from father before we would crash into the room and seek out the goodies from heaven.

We'd notice that Santa had been, eaten the cake and sipped the drop of whiskey. For years I could not understand how Santa managed to come down the chimney and not leave a speck of soot. But then he is Santa, superman for a night, until his broad frame, sleek sleigh and tireless reindeers disappear into the night sky to re-appear the following year; the only racing certainty in the steeplechase of life.

This was a time when television had not taken hold of our leisure, so the morning would be spent with the sound of radio in the background as the bells for religious services of various denominations would toll from the

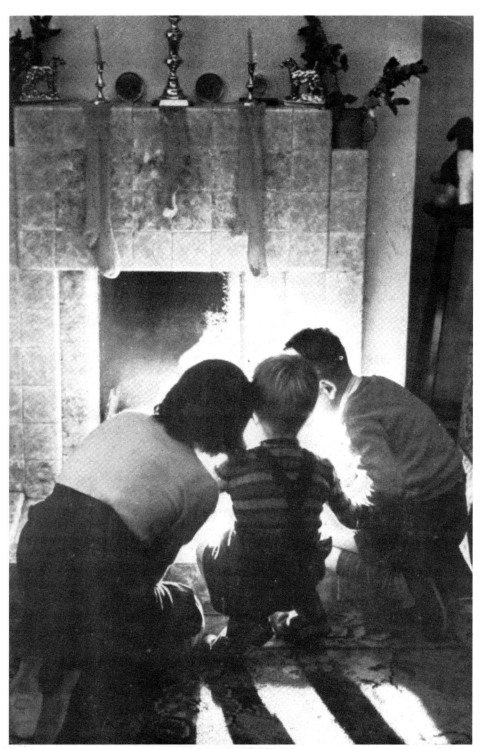

Great expectations

old Pye in the corner.

There was a sound from that radio like no other. As we grew older the dial was invariably hovering around 208 on the medium wave where Radio Luxembourg first suggested that Europe would one day shrink to its present size and our protected way of life would soon end. The advent of national television would change the old ways of Christmas days forever.

But that was then, and in the meantime, we would lie on the floor playing soldiers with the Horse Cavalry mounted on shiny black steeds. Dutifully they clip clopped along the marble fire-place and took up positions against the brother's set of Red Indians.

It never concerned us that they were not destined to meet in real life; our war games ignored international boundaries and the only injuries were bloody noses when territories were not observed and somebody pulled the rug from under charging troops.

Christmas day was one for spending entirely with immediate family and there was little or no traffic on the roads. Dad would want us to go for a walk to work up an appetite for the turkey dinner but we'd find an excuse and he'd go for a short walk alone.

Mum would be in the tiny kitchen from where the glorious aroma had wafted from early morning. There would be a rush of heat into the drawing-room when she opened the door of the oven to turn the bird. We'd 'bags' the legs, but age was honourable and we seldom succeeded. In later years, the legs would be left cool and we'd have a chew that evening, stuffed and all as we were. There is no taste as good as cold, brown turkey meat sprinkled with salt and an accompanying cup of tea.

The youngest would be relegated to a side-table which had its compensations as mother always made sure we got extra helpings. By evening the adults would be asleep in large chairs and we'd wonder why we did not feel so good. We'd finish the last chocolates in the box and then go off to bed, satisfied but wondering why the elders had become so nostalgic and wistful about another Christmas Day coming to an end.

THE OTHER SIDE OF CHRISTMAS

In adulthood and looking back there is a realisation that all too soon Christmas mornings become very quiet and very uneventful. There is then the other side of Christmas. I'm convinced that a handbook on the hazards inherent in the season would be a bestseller and I might write it myself. If we were to heed the admonition on the need to prepare ourselves spiritually in Advent, our morale might not be so low when Christmas arrives at our door.

First portent of the storm on the horizon is when she-who-must-be-obeyed suggests its time to get the tree. Now I'm totally against the idea of cutting down a perfectly healthy sapling, sticking it in a tub-full of earth and rocks and wrapping it in decorations akin to coloured toilet rolls. I know that there are excellent tree-holders on the market, and, to my surprise, I found the one we bought last year. Well, actually, the head of the house found it, having put it away carefully last January. So having forked out the £12 for the tree the next step was to place it in its stand. Now, how was I to know that the trunks of trees differ? I thought they were custom built. The tree was removed to the yard and much to the delight of the two dogs and the children, the chopping began. An hour later the tree stood, somewhat lopsidedly, with a decidedly bare look to its lower regions.

Now, Christmas lights! I just love the sweet moment of realisation that keeping the lights in a biscuit tin is possibly not the best way to ensure lighting-up time the following year. However, in this instance, Dad was brushed aside and daughter simply plugged them in to the socket. 'Marvellous,' I thought, 'they switched themselves on.'

There is no doubt about it that television has transformed Christmas in the homes of Ireland. Why indulge in conversation when you can sit for hours on end, in a suitably glazed state, as one feature film after another passes before your unseeing eyes? I could have sworn I saw Willie Wonka and his chocolate factory and Mary Poppins slide by me but then I couldn't have, could I? They were on last year, the year before and the year before that ...

Of course, one does not have to be completely idle sitting there. With the minimum of effort one can find out where the children put the sticky sweets they did not like, once they had reached the soft centres. I would think that many armchairs would have similar substances attached and that first clinging feeling on fingers could mean that one had found them some days later. More easily encountered is the chocolate which has been left on the driver's seat of the car. This will be discovered too late once one's best slacks have been put on and he who is never obeyed is heading for that important post-Christmas reception. I've noticed that chocolate brown does not go well with charcoal grey!

I know that Little Women's Christmas was obviously named in pre-feminist days, but I think some thought could be given to getting hard-pressed parents a break from the ritual of Christmas. The whole affair is so obviously weighted in favour of children that unfortunate mothers and fathers are driven to distraction in just coping with their darlings' freedom from school over the most miserable weeks, weather-wise, of the year.

Mothers spend hours in steam-filled kitchens, basting turkeys and whipping cream, talking to walls like Shirley Valentines. Dads, apart from the odd game of golf, lie prostrate on floors as the 'injuns' attack from all sides. At times like these, hours at the office do not seem so bad after all.

I've exaggerated the negative aspects. There are smiling, innocent faces on that first visit to the crib on Christmas morning; the peals of joy and ringing laughter as Santa's visit on that blessed night is confirmed by squeals of delight round that same tree. There is the not insignificant thought that Christmas is really the only time of the year when whole families are truly together.

LISTENING TO THE SILENCE

It was New Year's Eve ... The old lady was alone. Over the open fire the blackened pot hung; little droplets of water touched, then spat and hissed hot on the ashes of wood and turf. The tall clock, across the stone farmhouse floor, tick-tocked unseen in the December evening gloom. She listened to silence and remembered sounds of the past.

She could hear it now; it must have been a Christmas Eve and it was probably market day as the trap had been gone all morning from the haggard. Every market day the pony was brought in from the sheltered, three-cornered field at the back of the orchard and harnessed to the trap. Great slabs of home-made, salted butter would be wrapped in muslin, and sheets of white paper placed on the floor of the trap underneath the buttered eggs, for the journey to town fifteen miles away. Business done – a barter of butter and eggs for other provisions – it was home again, and normally the pony would be unhitched, watered and returned to the field.

Christmas Eves could be different as the pony and trap, if out that day, would be used again for Midnight Mass. Then the family would wrap up and huddle into the little trap which would rise up with the extra weight but settle again when the youngest would be brought up front to settle on Mum's lap.

Mass over, season's greetings exchanged in the frosted dark outside the church, it would be home again and a late supper of home-cooked ham on slices of brown bread and mugs of mother's soup, simmering since they had left the house a few hours earlier.

Off to bed for the children, after a decade of the Rosary – a dispensation from the five because of the lateness of the hour and the night that was in it. There was another, more cogent reason; Santa came early in those parts so the scatter up the stairs to the bedrooms had a purpose.

Mother and father sat on either side of the fire, and, here, another dispensation; a double drop of the dew for dad and mother settled for a teascán of the licit stuff with water. She would be inveigled, she remembered fondly, to take the Christmas cake out of its tin for the first time and there would be a slice each. Then the bright red, paper-ribbon was carefully folded and put in the sideboard drawer for next year. The talk would be of the year, on its last legs, and the year ahead, with all its bright promise.

She woke from her sleep and felt the pain when she did not see her husband smiling across at her. She poked at the fire and was soon nodding off again. It was now a New Year's Eve in her reverie.

Living on the land, the turn of the year was a tangible thing. In the kitchen garden, at the back of the house a cluster of snowdrop and daffodil spears would have already pushed through the damp clay. In a few weeks the earth would start to stir itself and there would be talk of grain seed, the cutting of sciolláins and the cleaning of machinery in the shelter of the big barn.

Its big doors swung crazily outside now and the plough hadn't been used in years. A few hens had the run of the place; the old collie, who had once eaten the head of the Christmas turkey hanging in the cold house, had died the year the master had gone.

In her sleep she could almost touch and feel that sense of loss that year. He had gone on his usual trip to town but the pony had shied at a barking dog and a trap-wheel hit a rock, dislodged from the ditch. Her husband was thrown from the trap and never regained consciousness. A lifetime of achievement and love over in an instant. It was never quite the same on the farm then. The children had long since scattered round the world.

The clock chimed the hour and a New Year was born. The old lady's hands hung loosely over the sides of the chair, the Rosary beads had fallen on the floor ... she felt no pain now.

A plane touched down at Shannon with her eldest daughter and two grandchildren on board ... about the time the neighbours found her. It was to be a surprise on that bright New Year's Day many years ago.

25

CHILDREN OF THE SNOW

When we were children, the fervent prayer was that it would never stop snowing and schools would close. We get cross now when our children storm Heaven for a similar happening.

At the first sign of a real snow-fall, we'd head for a hill beside a quarry which was only brilliant for bob-sleigh marvels. That same bob-sleigh would consist of a sheet of corrugated iron and two pieces of wood nailed underneath.

I'm very impressed when I see the real thing on telly now, as they hurtle down the run, but there was the same excitement when we launched from the top of the hill.

The skill was shown first in getting a running start which usually meant one of us ending up face down, as the rest, who had managed to stay on board, headed for the road below. It took a superior mind, and no little skill, to guide the rusting hulk along the track. The trick was then bringing it to a halt before it headed across the roadway. In those days a car was a fairly rare sight, so the danger was minimal, but the excitement was only mighty. Usually, the team would not reach the end but would have abandoned ship long before that.

A particularly sweet memory concerns one of those severe snaps when a little pond, in a recently flooded field in our parish, froze over and formed an ice rink which would have pleased Torvill and Dean.

There was something very romantic about those few days as young gallants held their sweethearts hands and every slip brought them closer together. Remember we are talking about a time when any chance we had to mix with the opposite sex was grabbed and much appreciated. When the thaw came, young love melted too because there was no chance of holding hands without the cloak of valour.

Strange all the same how, when we grow older and dread slippery footpaths, that this very scene was once our playground. Now we wrap up and wonder how another generation could be so fearless and foolhardy.

How easily we forget what harum-scarums we were, when the world stopped at the end of the street and our leisure centres were open fields. I wonder where all the snows of yesteryear are gone.

The battle of the bandstand

LAND OF THE RISING SUN

The finest cup of tea I ever drank was on the sunny side of a bale of straw after a day's threshing on the farmland of a family friend, forty years ago in sweet Ardho, Ardmore, Co. Waterford.

The runner-up was supped many years later in the Glen of Aherlow after a clash of the ash in Semple Stadium, Thurles.

Another contender for the title – 'all time great cups of tea' – was imbibed in the land of the rising sun, a few miles off the main road to Kinsale. It was savoured by the boot of the car after a few hours foot-beagling; it was nectar of the gods, a creamy pint would not have gone down as well.

The night of rain revealed a blue sky and glinting sun, only the crisp north-westerly stung the eyes and ears and reminded the gathering at the cross-roads that it was the First Sunday in January.

The first thing which struck me about the beagles was their size; compact and well-muscled but much smaller than their harrier cousins. The huntsman sounded his horn, the whips crackled in crisp air and it was over the bracken-brown topped fence, carefully along the boundaries of a field of winter wheat and down ploughed fields, funnelling to a bog of squelching clay and boot-sucking mud.

For the first hour or so I had no difficulty in keeping up with the hounds but as the day went on I realised, with some relief, that the pack did not take a straight line but came full circle, as it were; a scent in the air would bring them back through careful handling by the huntsman. Thus, it was possible to remain on some high ground and watch the proceedings a few fields away. I gained a new admiration for the few hares seen that day. They literally ran a drag with the hounds, lying in the form until the most opportune moment to sweep across the open countryside, sometimes bringing the entire pack over land already traversed and throwing confusion on top of a fleet of foot which has to be experienced at close quarters to be fully appreciated.

I hauled myself through a deep ditch to be told that the hare had passed along there minutes before, padding over the water for over thirty yards which astounded even the more seasoned beaglers.

I lost contact with the main party as the sun slipped to winter rest, bathing the land in a golden glow as the biting wind asserted itself once more and bones began to stiffen as the trudge back to the car began for those whose legs could take no more.

Huntsman and whips brought the pack back, muddied and exhausted. After careful counting they were put into their covered trailer and brought back to the kennels. In the inevitable chat in the local bar after the day out there was much talk of the quality of the hunt and genuine expressions of admiration for the performances of the hound and hare. As darkness came down I was glad those beautiful animals had the countryside to themselves.

Brandy and ice – footbeagle Brandy encounters his first snowfall

RANDOM THOUGHTS FROM THE TERRACES

In the 1950s, rugby brought my future wife and myself together. We won the Cup that day, that is Pres won the Cup. We (my wife and myself) were still at school then so we'd go our separate ways, but would marry some ten years later. I suppose that would be classed as a sort of sporting double. I wonder how many marriages have been first intimated on the terraces at Thomond Park?

February is grab-a-rug-from-the-boot-of-the-car, fill-up-the-hip-flask time of the year. Rugby internationals are, for some, about seeing and being seen. It's the corporate thing to do and I have noticed that Croke Park, on All Ireland days, are taking the rugby bods' line. Sport is very big business and the interest of the media ensures that those with a message, something to sell, want to be where all the attention is; 'good for business, old boy'.

There is that extra appeal about a rugby international which attracts even the lukewarm follower who would not stand for five minutes at a league match in Musgrave Park or Landsdowne Road.

Then there are the genuine followers of the game, not of fashion, who plan their year, from season to season, and can be seen in Murrayfield, Cardiff Arms Park or Twickenham roaring Ireland on and later recalling other encounters which they have attended down through the years. In the hostelries of Cardiff, London, Edinburgh, Paris and Dublin on match eves, rugby fans hold forth and defy all-comers on their knowledge and the depth of their passion for the oval-ball game.

Of course, with each pint, memorable tries become even more memorable and the speed of former players increases remarkably. It matters not that this or that try was not quite so spectacular; that a famous penalty was kicked, not from inside the kicker's half, but from just outside the twenty-five. Record books can be checked, but the story is all the better for the bit of exaggeration and those present are only half listening anyway.

Internationals always throw up some great moments and we all have our magic moves to warm the dark evenings.

There are those who will recall Cobh's J. C. Daly crashing over the Welsh line at Ravenhill in 1948 to give Ireland their first Triple Crown since 1899. Sadly, the great J. C. did not play for Ireland again. Ireland would win another Triple Crown in 1949.

There would be another long wait for another Triple Crown when Tom Kiernan would coach Ireland to a championship and Crown victory in 1982. Kerryman Mick Doyle would manage the last in 1985, Ciaran Fitzgerald captained both sides and with Tom's nephew, Michael Kiernan, getting the Triple Crown winning drop goal against England.

Other random moments would be the performance of the great Jack Kyle one year when he led the French a merry dance and prompted one Sunday newspaper to wax poetical ...

They seek him here, they seek him there ...
those Frenchies seek him everywhere ...
that paragon of craft and guile,
the damned elusive Jackie Kyle.

Then there were all those last gasp tries which sent us into ecstasy or depression, depending on who had scored and in which direction he was travelling.

There would be all those years we went to Cardiff with just the Red Devils to beat and we were caught. But then there was that glorious Saturday when the late Jerry Walsh crash-tackled Wales out of the game on that hallowed turf; there was no singing in the valleys that night and the performance of the former Pres, UCC, Sunday's Well star will never be forgotten by those who know their rugby.

In the early 1970s squash was about to go into orbit and in 1973 an international at Fitzwilliam on a Friday night brought me to Dublin. It happened that there was an international rugby match on the following day. It was no ordinary game, as the events which had preceded it were of particular relevance.

It will be remembered that Wales and Scotland had decided that Dublin in 1972 was no longer a safe place to play and there was a fear that the international rugby matches would not resume in Ireland for some time, because of the spill-over of troubles in the north.

I have a vivid recollection of journeying from Fitzwilliam late on the Friday night and seeing the steel barriers being placed in O'Connell Street. There was a tangible air of tension in our capital city and it was not all similar to previous rugby eves.

The Saturday was blustery and cold as we walked through security lines around the ground. It was the first time that this country had witnessed such careful vetting of fans.

It was only inside the ground there was growing realisation that the afternoon would be something special. England ran on to the Landsdowne turf to a deafening roar of welcome and the championships had been saved. Rugby followers have never forgotten that day and there is a genuine respect for the white shirts since then.

That was the year of the French too. They were special favourites in Dublin because in 1972 they made up for the loss of the Welsh and Scottish matches by playing us twice, and they always performed with Gallic flair and passion, although they did not always travel well. Their supporters always made an impression and I have one painful memory of an exuberant gentleman putting his foot on my breakfast plate in a Dublin hotel on the morning of a match.

It was nothing other than fervour which prompted him to do a dance on the table and, as he was about six foot four, I decided that I liked scrambled eggs anyway. It was his kisses of abject apology which were harder to take!

They say that the Welsh do not travel well but they are a wonderfully emotional people and must be feeling decidedly low at their recent misfortunes. I remember one year the lads in green over-ran the red devils and I was full of the joys of victory until I saw a lone, be-leeked figure sitting on the terrace steps as the rain torrented down. We struck up a conversation and he told me he had been travelling to Ireland since the previous Wednesday and thought it would be another few days before he'd be back in his native valleys. He was a miner and his entire holidays were spent following his team around for the championships. He had never even spoken to a player but knew what they had for breakfast. His whole life caved in when they were down and I can imagine his depression now.

My young friend on the terrace was not at all consoled when I recalled the times when the Welsh would rout the Irish every year. He had never seen play, but heard his father speak of such greats, down through the years, as Hayden Tanner, Bryn Meredith and Cliff Morgan. Morgan would become a BBC sports chief and one of the truly marvellous after-dinner speakers in the sporting world.

My Welsh fan's own heroes were the then youthful Gareth Edwards and Phil Bennett. He was heart-broken too, when Barry John left the scene, but good out-halves seemed then to grow on trees over there. The last time I ever saw your man with the leek, he was sitting outside a pub, looking as if he was about to leap into his pint.

We had our heroes too. Who will ever forget the jink of Kyle, the flying passes of John O'Meara, the strength of Noel Henderson and incredible power-house play of the late Gordon Wood from Garryowen?

The modern game is all about professionalism, New Zealand, Australia and South Africa dominate with the French and English not too far behind. These are hard times for Scotland, Wales and little Ireland.

It seems a long time ago (the 1960s) when we'd take the All-In from Cork to Dublin, be served coffee and biscuits on boarding; eat a fine lunch, alight at Landsdowne and have a slap-up dinner of steak and chips on the journey home. And all that for £2 return with a wax candle in the shape of a rugby ball thrown in. Those were the days.

Pres and Christians – muddied but unbowed at the Mardyke, Cork

DECORATED FOR BRAVERY

I'm a sucker for spring. The sun shining on my back ... nature's jump-leads at my shoulder-blades. St Bridget's Day! – Bridget must have been one of the first Christian feminists. A strong, fair-minded woman, principled. Her day is a harbinger of renewal, rebirth and leaving of winter's womb.

Of course, we are all creatures of habit, and it is no harm at all that we are lulled into a false sense of well-being about the future. A flash of light across a sullen sky and we search for the spade and fork; wonder where we put the autumn bulbs; fume when the lawnmower will not start and the bag of cement for the new patio has turned to granite.

The garden shed is a repository of our lost horizons. We swore in October we'd be organised this year. We'd go for long walks in winter to tune up for the longer days, but only developed cramp in the television remote control finger.

Things will be different this year, I told the family as I slumped in the big chair. This year we will meet the world head-on; there will be no turning back and this hibernation would be short-lived. They slipped out of the room one by one and I changed channel without even noticing it.

That's the problem with spring. It exposes somnolent corners of the mind where cobwebs find the living easy. There is that sense of renewal which spells trouble for the unfortunate who thinks DIY stands for Don't Injure Yourself.

Changing one's lifestyle should be a measured affair. There is no point in rushing things. I have been known to become decidedly dizzy standing on a footpath so the ascent to a ceiling by step-ladder would merit the Sherpa Tensing award for amateur decorators.

Those who know, and they emerge from the bubbles in your pint when you mention the subject, always suggest that the good work must not commence without first ensuring that the right equipment is to hand. There are two categories of self-aid decorators; those who clean their brushes after each job and those who leave the bristles to harden in the jam-jar on the frosted windowsill.

I tried rubbing the offending instrument against a garden wall but took the easy way out and bought another brush which turned out to be marvellous value at 99p. Lesson one, then, is clean your brushes after use – this writing is taking a serious turn.

'She who must be obeyed' suggested that, in order to paper the walls, I would first have to do the paint-work. To the experienced, this multi-tiered operation would present no problems, but, after several hours of rolling back carpets, shifting furniture and putting the ladder in place, the lid was still fast on the paint tin and I made the most constructive move of the day, I put on the kettle for a cup of tea.

As I sat atop this island of tables and chairs, the enormity of the job before me began to sink in. I took my courage in my hands and stood at the base of the ladder, seconds from a possible attack of vertigo, as I swatted a 'highly deadly black tarantula' from its webbed lair. If you have to emulsion the ceiling do not use white, opt for a more definite colour, otherwise you will, after a half an hour, find yourself, Laurence of Arabia-like, squinting at a desert of light. I spent several minutes daubing away a particularly stubborn crack in the ceiling only to find that it was a hair-bristle on a lens of my glasses.

The secret of painting objects which move when pushed is to ensure that you develop an instant recoil system. The brush, poised at the door panel is, when an energetic five-year-old pushes through in his defence of his transformer world against an equally low flying six-year-old, a recipe for disaster. But then the flying pot of paint will do wonders for that rather plain carpet.

Now, there are painters and paper hangers. Papering is a real art about which I claim to know very little. The mixing of paste – always add the water and not the other way round – is a great domestic ritual not to be conducted when the nerves are bad. The secret is constant stirring and the eye of a good confectioner in its preparation.

Getting the paste to the paper is done with a broad emulsion brush; getting the paper to the wall is the stuff of great home movies. As you climb the ladder with the paper wrapped around your head and shoulders, spare a thought for those who built the pyramids. As you put your foot through the paper, remember the end result of your efforts could place you with the gods in the eyes of your fellows. As you chase the bubbles of air and try to hang your work of art, the thought must cross your mind that papering over life's cracks is best left to those who know something about it ... politicians.

Roses are red, violets are blue

St Valentine's Day and that first delicious realisation that there might be more to life than Cowboys and Indians. So the merry-go-round of emotions will turn again for another generation of boys and girls who will be walking on air for days on end if that mysterious card, from that secret admirer, comes in the post, or as is more likely, is handed over by a third party on the way home from school.

One could go through an entire lifetime wondering who has sent what to whom. There must be the makings of a best-seller in the stories of how this or that couple first met and if their's was a meeting of hearts in early teens.

I would guess that there are more souvenir, first-love Valentine cards lying around than we would imagine. There is something about the anonymous declaration of ardour, scribbled on a hand-made card. Its emotional impact can never be equalled by more sophisticated missives. Many a mother has shed tears when a little son's declaration of passion, shoved under the bedroom door that very morning, made all the nappy changing, wiping of tears, dabbing of grazed knees, just years before, all worthwhile.

The first real Valentine always registered 10 on the love-scale. For days there would be the wonder of it all; that someone out there would think enough to write it, and then, the exquisite joy of guessing who was the sender. That we never found out was a further insurance for our ego. We could speculate as to the identity of the author. That it might have been posted by someone just for a laugh would never cross our minds.

Of course, love is not the preserve of the young. The malady is not selective and has been known to attack all ages, and unlike the flu, there has never been a vaccine to lessen its effects. Shakespeare wrote of the pangs of disprized love and commercial rhymesters have earned a fortune ever since.

Symptoms vary at the outset. The patient swings from trapeze of elation and discovery to the sawdust ring of disappointment when love swoops low or simply dies.

There is the teenager who takes an inordinate interest in parents' own first love, or indeed, their original meeting. This could be a child who has hitherto not shown the slightest notice of mum or dad, but has suddenly taken to gazing into space and emitting deep sighs, losing all interest in such minor activities as eating or sleeping.

Of course every generation feels that they hold the franchise on romance. In every school in Ireland, boys and girls spend quiet moments even in class time dreaming up exquisite admissions of love. They plan how they will be delivered through a sister or brother, never into the hands of parents.

In every age, how many cards are actually signed: Guess Who? How many young blades have never revealed to their beloved that they had written that first Valentine?

I wonder how many marriages made in heaven took their first earthly steps through a simple, unsigned Valentine card.

Now where did I put that pen and how do you spell ... undying ...?

The wild daisies pressed ...

STALIN'S VOICE IN THE WIND

I've never been quite ready for Lent. As a child, the thought of forty days of anything, other than that which passed for normal for a lad, carried some sort of threat.

I can recall spending time on deciding what exactly I should give up for the penitential season and then the same amount of time convincing myself that I did not really have to give up sweets or stop taking the odd puff from the buddy's Woodbine.

I remember once, in a grand gesture, deciding that I'd give up going out with girls. I was seven!

I can never think of Lent without hearing in the mind wind crying on the telephone wires. It seems now that an east wind, dark grey clouds, black and bitterly cold mornings, were part of the Lenten scene.

I remember too being really scared as a lad when a pal told me that if you listened carefully to the same east wind, you could hear the voice of Stalin. It had to do with a radio broadcast which said one morning that the easterly had swept from that vast land of Russia, then across continental Europe to our very doorstep.

I felt vulnerable. If Russia was a million miles away, how could we share the same wind? Unlike present generations, with instant global communication, we were not to know that people were basically the same all over the world, but Stalin, then, was synonymous with fear.

Coming back to those resolutions, there was something charmingly innocent about our offers of denial at such a young age. Take giving up sweets. It was not easy I can tell you. I know that now there are bars and bars of chocolate to tempt a saint, but we had to be of brave heart in our time.

As children we had our temptations too. Being off the sweets, we could still see those large jars with the twist-off tops, full of hard-boiled sweets, from acid drops to bullseyes, sticks of barley sugar and fruit lollipops. What was a child to do; ignore, leave the occasion of sin and offer it up? We did our best but we'd fail too and was it any wonder?

Then an old penny would buy a dozen wrapped toffees or a little brown paper bag of bon bons. I often wonder what saints in ancient times would have done. Giving up the fags was not quite so traumatic. Anyway, I was known to get sick after a few drags behind the wall. Also, Dad would spot brown fingers from a mile off and then I'd be in for it. That man was a saint, trying to keep up with us, but Mum was our supreme advocate when matters of keeping to the straight and narrow arose.

Remember gobstoppers ... yes ... gobstoppers? What! You've never heard of them? They are rotund confections which lasted, it seemed, for ever. You could buy a gobstopper, pop it in your mouth, hop on a bus, arrive in town and your only friend would still be rolling round the tongue and you in salivary heaven. It killed all conversation and it was, of course, contrary to all advice about healthy teeth, but nothing would deter the dedicated gobstopper eater.

Then there were lucky balls. These were pink lads which, if you were fortunate, would contain an old halfpenny. The trick was not to swallow it, but extract it, and hope for another because an old penny really travelled then. Then, for no reason at all, toffee-apples come to mind. I am delighted to see that they can still be found, particularly at carnivals and open-air events during what passes for summer on this island. There was something particularly pleasurable in biting through the hot caramel surface into the contrastingly bitter taste of the apple.

My own favourite were clove rocks. Yes, clove rocks. Now there was a taste to linger long after you had cracked the white outer shell and bitten into the red part. A clove rock had them all beaten though a penny's worth of acid drops could keep you going on a cold school morning.

There was the temptation to try one in class which was not at all conducive to good diction or for the delivery of Mark Anthony's declaration of love for Cleopatra. There was the innate skill in being able to open the paper bag while still in your pocket and run your hand across your mouth, as if in some grand oratorical gesture, as you slipped the sweet inside. There was a downside to all this, as removing half-forgotten sticky sweets from the inside lining of pockets called for great patience and no little skill before mother found out.

Now, hands up those who remember those little liquorice pipes. They were only gorgeous, with their little sprinkle of pink grains suggesting a lit bowl. As kids, we thought we were only great, walking round with these held to the mouth. We spend half our lives wishing we were adults and the other looking back on lost youth.

Then there were liquorice all-sorts and I'm sure they are still on the go. We'd buy them by the quarter pound. I'd pick out all the black and white ones and the black ones and leave the rest.

My generosity was always the subject of comment amongst friends. Better still, I'd swap the ones I did not like for the equivalent number of aniseed balls which were all the rage then.

Remember cough-no-mores? You surely do. I do not know if it was ever medically proven that you would cough no more, but they were only brilliant when taken in small doses as they were strong stuff, asking a friend to smell your breath following the first sweet hitting the tongue. On reflection, breathing on someone else was not very hygienic but real friendship always stood the test.

On Easter Sunday morning the east wind would always be gone.

CIRCLE OF SAWDUST IN THE MORNING RAIN

I was twelve years old when I first fell in love. There I was in Pres cap and blazer swearing I'd never love another and she was never to know it. It was an up in the clouds romance, she was a trapeze artiste and I was a smitten schoolboy.

That circus pitched its tent along the Mardyke, near the Cricket grounds, sometime in the 1950s. We skipped the last class to be on time for a matinee performance. It was the one and only time I was 'ar ealú ón scoil'.

I had seen her first wrapped round a lamp post ... on a poster. She had nice legs, I thought it was a sin to think that but they were lovely. A kindly confessor said it was all right once I did not take too much pleasure in it. Armed with the blessing of the Church, I kept my love to myself; no one would know about our romance, not even the lovely girl on the high wire.

It was a curious affair in another respect. There I was head over heels as she balanced above me and I had an abiding fear of heights. I could not bear to look up and could not look down because I was certain I'd fall between the seating – very hard to impress the girl of your dreams in that position.

The circus left town just hours after the tent had folded that night. All that was left the next morning was a circle of sawdust in the rain.

The teacher was not at all impressed with my reason for missing last class the day before but then he was not suffering the first pangs of love. I thought I'd never get over her loss but I did and have never failed since to be fascinated by a circus and its people.

The survival of the circus in modern Ireland is a remarkable story. It must be the hardest end of the entertainment business but continues, against all the odds, to give joy to generations of children in every corner of Ireland. There is a circus buff in all of us.

I was sad to hear once that a fire had damaged a section of circus equip-

When the circus came to town

ment up the country. I was not at all surprised that the word from the owners was that the show would go on that very night.

The Russians and Chinese have provided the great sawdust performers down the centuries and the Americans showbiz panache has to be experienced. I was fortunate to attend a performance of the combined Ringling Bros, Barnum and Bailey Circus in Madison Square Gardens in 1979 and it was an impressive three-ring affair.

Described as 'The Greatest Show on Earth' it paraded, simultaneously, the talents of the much loved clown Lou Jacobs and his little dog Knucklehead. Lou's daughter Dolly flew through the air with the greatest of ease on the Roman rings but the highlight for me was Gunther Gebel Williams and his performing tigers.

It truly was an extravaganza but because I sat so far up in the Garden that special intimacy, associated with our own smaller travelling troupes, was missing.

Another pleasant memory was the visit of Chipperfield and Bertram Mills to the Victoria Road site in Cork. At Gilabbey Rock, I think it was, Duffy's and Fossett's filled summer evenings with colour and laughter. It is marvellous to see another generation of those families, and others, still taking to the roads – cavalcades of magic on the highways of our lives.

TOP OF THE MORNING

Top of the morning to you and yours. Bhuil tú reidh? Every year our National Day is with us before we know it, and then we're really cruising into brighter days, at least that is our hope, it may be quite different.

I love St Patrick's Day, always have, ever since I was a toddler and looked up at the kitchen windowsill where the shamrock, still with wet clay attached to its roots, rested in a willow-patterned saucer of water to keep it fresh.

On the morning, mother would distribute little pieces, reserving the best for Dad and there would be great searching for pins to keep it on coats. Otherwise it would be pulled through the openings on suit lapels. Then it was off to Mass with us children rather self consciously patting down the sprig in case it was too ostentatious. We did not know what 'ostentatious' meant, but that was the way we felt. Funny how little things embarrassed us as children and yet we make no allowance when our own complain now.

My aunt had a lovely little shop and we had her heart scalded as we tried to climb up on the counter, pointing out what we wanted and generally disrupting commerce for the morning. When you are young you feel no one's needs are as great as your own, and on those Patrick's mornings, you would have been right. All the days of longings for something sweet would have to wait as we spent every brass farthing of our pocket money, saved during spartan days.

In our early teens the Patrick's afternoons were only heaven. We'd walk the then quiet road to Douglas Village. We would have arranged to meet girls from the city and local schools. That was real freedom not enjoyed during school term. The word 'macho' had not been invented but I suppose in our own little way we fancied ourselves as being gifts to womanhood, God help us.

Selling shamrock outside Woolies

In the stretched evenings, we'd stroll back to our homes and our co-education would be over for another few weeks at least until Easter when we'd promise to all meet again. The whole atmosphere was one of indolence and innocence in a time when life drifted sweetly by for those who had their whole lives before them.

Of course, I'm a sucker for parades and the first notes of a brass band coming down a city street will find me full of the joys of life. I can just see how people would march into battle behind a band. It has that kind of hypnotic effect and still has for me to this day. I love the city on parade day. Those lovely streets come into their own when the traffic is banned and whole families stroll around at their leisure. You would want the weather though to be standing and waiting for the floats to pass by.

Many a parent has come closer to his children on such days than perhaps at any other time in their growing up. It is as if the child senses that he or she is sharing with a parent a world which is largely reserved for adults, who spend the rest of the year suited and commercial. For just one day, we are casual and relaxed in the way children like us to be.

As we become engulfed in matters European there is a danger we could forget those features which make us that bit different. For twenty-four hours at least, we are Irish and have a quite distinct culture which sets us apart from the rest. The more Europe unifies, the more we need to be comfortable as ourselves.

Happy moments

I find Easter Saturdays somewhat unsettling. There is that curious sense of unease that Lent has not been well spent. The resolve was there at the beginning, but, much as mid-January reveals the chinks in the resolute armour of New Year's Day, Easter Saturday reflects the lack of effort which reaps its own rewards of that indefinable sense of lost opportunity.

Remember Lents with the wind-up of the Annual Retreat and the churches jammed to the doors? The first week was usually for the men and, on the final night, the wives and girlfriends would be waiting outside for their menfolk. Then there was the phenomenon of preacher-spotting when some churches would have a particularly brilliant speaker and that church would be full for the week. Then it would be, catch-a-bus to the city and see the latest film at the Savoy, the Pav, Palace, Lee, Ritz, Coliseum or Assembs. Remember the big films took ages to reach this part of the world, so there was a real excitement about going to the cinema. But the chat between the newsreels, cartoons and main feature was, inevitably, all about the missioner and what he had to say. The following week, notes would be compared.

I remember Easter Saturdays when we went to school until noon and then would be sent home early with the admonition to get to confession. Having made our peace with God, we lads would head for a quiet corner of a nearby field and would eat ourselves sick. The Lenten Fast had finished at noon and our accumulated pocket money would be spent on such exotic fare as penny bars, fizz bags, and peggy's legs.

Easter Sundays would begin with Mass and, on returning home, there would be something of the ritual of Christmas, with the man of the house distributing the Easter eggs which would have been hidden some weeks before. It says something for our sense of restraint that we children knew where they were all the time but did not go near them. More likely, of course, they remained untouched because we knew we would have to go without on the Sunday if we had gone near them. Some families had real boiled eggs with faces painted on them.

Nowadays, Easter eggs come in all shapes and sizes and with all sorts of attachments. They are a marketing dream but a nightmare for those who hold the purse-strings. We really have over-commercialised Christmas and Easter and lost somewhat the true meaning of the feasts.

Another happy memory of both St Patrick's Day and Easter Sunday was the annual trek to the 'merries'. Our visits will remain something special for me. There was no car in the family, so we'd walk the few miles and I can still recall the simple joy of climbing the hill, looking over the valley and picking out the colourful canopy of the chair-o-planes. If the wind was from the south-east, we'd hear the music too and there'd be a mad rush down the road in case we'd miss one marvellous moment in the bumpers or the penny ticket stalls. By six, we'd be wrecked, and, would barely make the journey back to a tea of scones and apple tart. If we had a shilling left we'd be out again the next day, Easter Monday.

Time and distance colour everything and it is true we recall best that which we enjoyed most in our lives. What we tend to forget is that each succeeding generation stores up its fond memories. Today's children are not any different and though they may appear to have more of the world's goods and are more sophisticated, it is still the simple joy of unwrapping an Easter egg, or the very first spin on the amusement park carousel as proud parents look on, which will warm their thoughts many years later.

Many years later my father-in-law said the sun danced in the sky on Easter Sunday mornings; true faith is a wonderful thing.

Burying dreams

'Mr Man, I found your onions.' It was a two-foot walking talking anorak informing me that my carefully laid shallot and onion bed had been uncovered. The dear child had wandered into the back garden, at the invitation of my three-year-old, who seemed to spend his days inviting other mites to 'play and kick ball' around, and generally near, my postage stamp vegetable patch.

'My Dad is a gardener,' boasted the same young host. 'He buries things and I find them like you did,' he explained to his lollipop-sucking friend.

Strange, isn't it, how normally sane people don old jerseys, socks and big boots, with trousers spotted with last year's paint and make like Percy Throwers – green fingers and all. A packetful of miracles – vegetables bursting out at you from their colourful seed sachets and flowers which dazzle red, white and blue and promise to smother that dark corner in a carpet of colour. I can now reveal, rather belatedly, that the lettuce clustered and bolted at a rate never mentioned in any gardening manual; the carrots, which I had earmarked for many a stew, disappeared into the ground and were eaten by some fly which everyone seemed to know about but myself.

Despite these setbacks I had turned the sod, as they say, and laid my plans for that bumper harvest. Now that child from God knows where, running nose and soulful eyes, stood there with a fistful of my onion bulbs sticking to his lollipopped hands. I counted ten and returned to the task.

'Can I help you, Dad?'

It was the heir apparent standing directly over the spot where I had spread the beetroot seed with numbed fingers.

'No, you cannot help, and would you and your friend ... play elsewhere?' I screamed.

His lower lip puckered a little but he still managed to look me straight in the eyes, as I knelt in supplication, and he informed me: 'I don't want to be a gardener anyways'. He turned on his little heels and hand-in-hand with his destroyer friend headed for the gate to bait some other unsuspecting adult.

It was then I noticed that the same beetroot packet pointed out that it was not advisable to set the seed in extreme cold. I consoled myself that I was really only in it for the fresh air and returned to the warmth of the house, pulled up a chair to the fire and dreamt of 'cabbages and kings'.

Digging up the present

MOVING ON

When I was a lad ... years ago, it seems now the sun always shone; it did not, but this far removed it appears that way. Blackrock was not the extended city it is now but rolling rurality from Beaumont to the Lough Mahon shore, the Marina to the Douglas River. Summer days were spent swimming in crystal clear Lough Mahon waters where the flotsam of modernity, plastic bags and rusting tin, now mark muddy waters. Autumns were crowded with slocking sorties to walled orchards, including my grandfather's, and there was the drone of threshing machines.

We were poor in the sense that we did not have life's luxuries, nor did we want for them. Television was something the British had and a video machine was not necessary as we had no need to record what was passing when the next fun-filled moment was the only thing that counted.

I have one particularly happy memory of heading for the Atlantic Pond, jam-jar in one hand and fishing net on a bamboo stick in the other. The half mile journey from home was everglades stuff. Not for us the obvious route up the main road when we could tramp through the growth of the derelict railway line.

Then the undergrowth had reclaimed the line so progress was slow for the file of us youngsters who could imagine tigers in the bush and a raiding party of Indians from the city. Life was lived for us Cowboys with danger in every stride but we never came to harm in those gentle, short pants days.

The Pond safely reached, we'd sit on the little bridge at the Athletic Grounds end and discuss the hours of angling which lay ahead. I can still see it as if it was yesterday. The little stream which filtered into the entrance channel to the pond, carried thousands of little silver tawneens (thorneens, if you were not from the village). They were perfectly formed little fish who were almost small enough to slip through the fine mesh of our nets but, once in the jar and looked at through the glass, they were magnified and marvellous, held aloft for the adult passers-by to admire. One of the gang always maintained that they were young salmon and who were we to argue.

The journey home was always by public road so that the world could see our catch for the day. There was a grey cat in our backyard who would interrupt his siesta on the flat roof to extricate the unfortunate fish. It did not matter, there always was another sunny day when we were young.

The gang are men now, scattered round the world with cares greater than who would catch the most fish and still be home, starving but satisfied that the hours were well spent. Sure, who would worry about anything when you thought nothing would ever change, no one would ever move on.

Another time ... another place – Ardmore in the sunshine of our happy youth

The day an angel fell in the pond

Funny the things you remember about your childhood. Stranger still the events which pass from the memory leaving no residual effect unless others recall them. First Communion and Confirmation Days loom large for parents and the participants.

I don't know about now but in my time we were preparing, it would seem, for months for the great day. The local priest would visit and see that we had some idea of what it was all about. Young though we were, we did have that sense of occasion and a genuine belief in the importance of it all.

Credit then to our teachers who must at times have despaired of ever inculcating us with sufficient knowledge to get us through. It was all learning by repetition but, if you think about it now some of those little prayers and bits of information on matters eternal stayed in the mind. They rush to the surface when we face some sort of crisis when only prayer, however brief and emotionally superficial, will get us through until normal service is restored.

We would all have memories of those special days and I thought I might share with you a recollection of my Communion Day when things went slightly wrong.

It was a glorious Saturday and I recall, as if it was yesterday, the walk down the road with my parents to the church. Curiously, the ceremony is not all that clear with me but I would have to say that receiving the Host for the first time was something special. We were no angels but I suppose for a few short minutes our proud parents must have thought we were. There we were, little figures sitting in the front seats, our heads plastered down with hair-oil, pictures of cherubic innocence.

Being in a convent school and a small class, after the ceremony we were brought to a lovely warm room with grand big furniture and given a fry breakfast. I can taste the rashers and eggs still and see the sun shining through the great windows as we sat on soft chairs and decided that growing up might not be too bad after all.

Later we would stroll around the grounds and that is where this particular angel lost his wings. There is something of a show-off in most of us, given half a chance. When you are very young the temptation to impress contemporaries is strong. Nothing would do but for me to take a walk on the wild side and do a balancing act on the surround of the fish pond. Yes, you guessed it, I slipped and ended up sitting in the pool as the goldfish shot for cover under the lily pads.

I do not know if you were dressed to the nines for your great day but I know my mother and father had gone to great trouble to deck me out in Sunday best even though it was Saturday. My suit was ruined. It was one of those lovely grey ones with matching long socks and black patent shoes all shiny and bright.

The ensemble was complete with red tie, white shirt and a medal pinned to the lapel. Well they were, but now I was almost totally covered in water and silt dredged up by my fall. I cannot recall what was said to me but not for the first time my parents showed restraint and calm in the face of great provocation. They were the real saints on that day, as always.

My parents – saints in their day

LITTLE WORLD CUP

There was a big field in Ballinsheen, Blackrock, corralled by a stone wall. It was short grass country in my time as a lad. It became an overgrown South Fork and sometimes home for wild horses before industry had its say. Our gang were never great at field games but the terrible alternative was to face the opposition in a game of Cowboys and Indians in nearby Bessboro Walk. We would always opt for a little World Cup in soccer rather than suffer the ignominy of slipping home after dark, our feathers ruffled and war-paint (mother's lipstick) smudged. Not great either on the field of play, we were fierce entirely for the pre-match tactics. You could say we were ahead of our time.

Just before the big game would begin, after the pitch had been prepared by the home side (coats for goals and stones to mark the sidelines), our team would clear a wall behind the city goal and rush on to the pitch. The object of this exercise was to confuse the opposition into thinking that there were fewer of us than there was of them.

Our manager believed that movement was sound business. Just before the kick-off or throw-in, depending on the code, there would be some smart-ass on the other side who would call for a count, but, bustle was the name of the game and the match would have begun by the time he latched on to the fact that we had more players than our more fancied opponents.

Another interesting ruse on our part was to play all the small fellows in the back-line and the smallest of all in goal. The thinking was that our opponents would feel sorry for the size of the defence and go easy on them while our bigger fellows would be knocking them in up front. So much for tactics. I don't think we ever won a match.

Many a jersey I left behind in the darkness as it had doubled for goal-posts. I'd tell me Ma but never Da.

OUR PLAYGROUND

There is a highway now where we sported and played. I wonder what our auto route users from other countries make of us as they speed by. They will not know that in the 1940s, 1950s and even 1960s, that whole area was our playground.

Summer-time came easy then in Blackrock when we'd walk or bike to the Yanks. Past Ballinsheen Cross, over the old Blackrock/Passage Railway bridge by the quarry full of turf which lit many a fire during the war. Smoke from open fires spiralled upwards in the country air. Down the narrow, briar-lined lane we'd go and we'd be in the Yanks by ten in the morning – on our 'holiers' and by the sea. 'Crosser' could have been Tahiti for all we knew.

We'd swim all day in crystal clear waters. Then we'd lie in the sun on the warm side of the wall which is still there at the end of the big field, just near the point of the western tunnel entrance and exit.

Home in the late afternoon then, through lovely Ballinure. I often think of other spots too given exotic names such as Dodge City and White City. Now it is hard to trace the old route home as any kind of progress has its price too. Those once empty fields have factories which provide vital jobs and good living for some of the people of the area. All that road and tunnel building means hundreds of jobs. That is how things go and time certainly marches on, as the old newsreel would say.

Still it's nice to now and again switch on the best video of all, the memory, and recall times and places not yet beyond recall.

I mentioned happy days down the 'Walks' where the 'Battle of Little Big Horn' and 'Custard's (we always thought it was 'Custard', it spoiled it a bit to find it was plain Custer) Last Stand' was played over and over again. History would be re-written and the US Cavalry would win, much to the annoyance of the 'injuns' amongst whom I was usually numbered. I was small and you played on the side your betters decided for you.

I remember one particularly intense battle which was abandoned when the foot soldiers went home to tea. Snag was I was still tied to the oak tree doubling as a totem pole and would be there still if an adult had not seen my problem. I never said anything about it to the others as I would have been shot at dawn for insubordination. You see the next day I was picked for the Cavalry as a kind of Indian scout.

My duties were to sit on a branch of a tree and tell the rest playing below when the enemy would be seen crossing the Douglas River which was of course, the Delaware. Then there was the Black Bridge (it was red) which had no planks on it, so getting to the other side was a precarious business which I never had the heart to negotiate. I found early on in life that cowards tended to live longer.

It was not all Cowboys and Indians as each season suggested its own activities. Autumn weeks, all those years ago, would have been taken up with a quick dash after school to gather nuts. Yes, none of your shop stuff in net bags for us, we were after the real thing and nature was bountiful.

I cannot remember all their names, but there were walnuts and hazel-nuts. The fun with walnuts, if that was what they were, was cracking the outer shell. When we would exhaust other methods, such as banging them between two stones, we'd raid a kitchen belonging to one of the lads and use the nut-cracker. I do not know if they are used now but I'm sure there are a few well-rusted in the undergrowth down the walks to this very day.

When we got a bit older we would play other games which were in themselves an admission that we had noticed that there were girls in the world. Up to this it was a little men's paradise. When they did come into our lives nothing would ever be the same again. A game of 'release' was the height of our early teen ambitions ... sure we were the innocent souls.

FIELD OF DREAMS

There was always a hurley in the house. You'd find one in the back porch, at the end of the long hall, in the big hall-press and if it was a really good one, seasoned and well flasked with a good 'bas' for left or right striking, then it could be found under the bed of its sleeping owner.

A good hurley to a hurler was as precious as the fiddle to the musician from Doolin although, as recent history confirms, they are no mean judges of a hurley in the Banner either.

Hurling was everything to us as children. Though schooled in the great rugby nursery Pres on the Western Road in Cork and a fairly fanatical supporter myself of our efforts against great rivals Christians, my first love was hurling.

When we were growing up there was hardly a car on the road and we were ahead of our time as the constant game was beating a lawner against the house and doubling on it in the opposite direction against the old natural stone boundary wall behind. We never broke a window but there would be a tap on the glass from Mum to warn us that Dad was on his way from work and we'd stop play for the day.

That said, Dad loved to see us with a hurley in our hands and I can remember as if it was yesterday his marching us down to the Athletic Grounds of a Sunday to see the Rockies playing against the Glen, the Barrs or Sars. We'd stuff our short-pants pockets with apples from the orchard and off with us up the main road, down Barrington's Avenue and along the Atlantic Pond to the pitch where now stands Pairc Uí Chaoimh.

Dad would bring us into the sideline which consisted of great planks of wood stretched between then rotting supports and underneath was a little drain. If the plank gave way or one got carried away with excitement, then there was a squelch and Sunday shoes and pants would be destroyed.

The man from Cloyne, who played with the Glen, the incomparable Christy Ring, was my father's idol when he wore the rebel red of Cork but

Waterford's Ned Power takes flight with sliothar in hand as Cork's maestro Christy Ring thunders into the square

my father's tune changed when the Ringer played with the Blackpool side. That was understandable as club rivalry is the impetus which keeps Gaelic games alive at the all-important grassroots level. The day professionalism comes in, watch that fervour being blown away.

I played the game very much at grassroots level. To be honest I was no great shakes at the game; more a theorist which did not account for much when you had to tog off for an Under Age match at the side of a ditch and put a stone on your clothes for fear they would be blown away as the wind swept over the old pitch at Kilbarry when we'd play away.

Those were the days when Blackrock played in the top pitch, above the hockey grounds, later the AUL soccer pitches, now a suburban estate, in Church Road. The club rose to an old wooden railway container which acted as a dressing-room and you can imagine the excitement when we'd all pile into this before the match. Half of us would not get on the first fifteen but the mentors, bless them, would say: 'Tog off, you'll all be on; you'll all get a game.'

And if we were winning well we would all get a run and many a happy day I ran onto the pitch with Number 25 on my back but I did not care. All I knew was that I was wearing the green and gold and nothing else mattered; not even if I did not get a puck of a ball.

Two of my older brothers were very handy; one playing with Ballinure and the other excelling in soccer and rugby and winning a Senior County medal with Blackrock in 1956.

My only claim to fame was when my younger brother and myself figured on the Marian Park team in 1954. This was at the vital Parish League level and we ended up taking the last trophy to be won on that pitch as the move across the road to Blackrock's present splendid complex took place around then.

The old GAA pitch bordered on its west side by the stone wall near the Huts in Beaumont was our field of dreams.

Recurring nightmares

Ever noticed how particularly traumatic happenings of one's childhood can surface much later in life and come to haunt when least expected? I was not a particularly brilliant student, as any of my teachers still on this earth will readily agree. It was not so much that I was a dull student, in fact I was particularly inventive, not at all short on imaginative flights which defied textbook education and belied my poor showing at exam time.

Of course, the class had its usual share of genius and I suppose the ultimate test was that all managed to find our way in the world without too much difficulty. That was more a tribute to the labours of our teachers and their belief that knowledge, just a little, will stick if thrown in the direction of the student hard and often enough.

My education could be said to be phased. I thought initially that once you reached First Year that it was the equivalent of receiving the key to freedom from responsibility of any kind. It was only when I stumbled into Inter. Cert year that I realised that there is more to life than the girls' school across the river and those marvellous days in Limerick and Rockwell when we carried the flag for the rugby team. We always seemed to win then and victory half-days gave us even more time to polish up our skills at pontoon, pitch and toss and knuckles, or gobs under the shade of a tree which still stands in Fitzgerald's Park on the Dyke.

By the time Leaving Cert came round, phase two of my education was in progress and there was a new discipline in my life. 'Eckers' were completed on time and not cobbled together five minutes before first class in the school toilet. I think it was the first year in twelve that I managed to arrive at school every day with a textbook for each class which became something worthy of comment in the staff room. God bless the teachers that year, they pulled me through the Leaving, defying all logic and no doubt causing puzzlement in the Department of Education.

And that brings me to the nightmares first suffered in my teens. Weeks before the actual exams dementia set in and I'd wake up, having been confronted in my sleep with an exam paper which bore no resemblance to the course set.

Mathematics was my weakest subject and special tuition after hours, grinds for grinds, and hours of pencil chewing, biro biting, did little to lift the veil on its intricacies.

My maths teacher deserved a medal that year as I know now that he despaired of me being even able to read the questions, not to mind answer them, but he never let me know this. God bless the man, now gone to his deserved reward in heaven, he kept telling me, have faith in him and he would get me at least a pass. He did, but not without cost to his equanimity. I'm certain that he considered my 40 pass mark as the equivalent of the splitting of the atom. Certainly, there was as much energy expended in the process. Anyway I still wake in the cold sweat and that dream of being unable even to read the paper still resurrects itself every now and again and the heart is beating just as fast when I eventually wake.

Model students

No business like show business

I can never think of summertime without remembering shows of yester-year when we'd get out of school for a half-day or get some part-time work in the show-grounds when classes closed for the summer. It seems now that the sun always shone, which of course it didn't, only that we have the capacity to disremember that which is not to our liking. If we had trouble rising each morning for school there was no difficulty at all when show days dawned. Myself and the pals would be down outside the gate of the grounds in Ballintemple before they were open and it was all go 'til evening time.

You will have your own memories of those days but here are a few of mine. Being city lads, we were not exactly experts on the equine breed but I was always stuck by the sheer height of the animals as they backed out of their boxes and would later trot around the enclosure at judging time.

There was a great air of dignity and attention to detail with the animals in beautiful condition and their handlers in full regalia sitting erect, keeping control with the merest movement of the reins. I never knew what separated the winner from the rest but I always felt that to be a judge was special and very much in the adult domain for those of us in short pants and rubber dollies.

On then to the inner halls where the various stands proclaimed their products and if you think about it those firms were much ahead of their time. We'd gather leaflets from almost every stand and felt very important as we hurried along, not exactly rubbing shoulders but at least on the same level as captains of industry who did whatever was done at these shows. I know that they showed inestimable patience with us youngsters but we were part of the show days and would all too soon grow up ourselves.

I remember Thompsons had a restaurant in one corner of the ground and we'd wait around there in the hope that some relation might spot us, treat us to lemonade and those gorgeous snowball cakes which made a high tide mark around your lips and your nose would be tipped with cream after each bite.

In the afternoon we'd get into the jumping enclosure which, to lads who had never been to even a gymkhana, and had not yet encountered that great killer of the youthful inquisitiveness, the television, would provide hours of excitement as we sat up in the open stand which adjoined the old covered one.

All eyes would swivel to the enclosure in a corner at the Blackrock end as the bowler-hatted announcer and judges would take up their position in the centre, which I think was a raised, glass-encased podium.

I remember the names of Captain Harry Freeman Jackson and Iris Kellett and the huge cheer which could be heard in the hills of Montenotte when a clear round was achieved.

In the evening sunshine we would make our way home and offer to sell all the booklets and pamphlets to our parents. Our entrepreneurial talents had already been awakened.

Parade of the champions

HOME ALONE

When I was a lad I loved the month of June. School was nearly over and we had just the summer exams to negotiate before the bell would ring for last class and there would be ... 'no more Latin, no more French, no more sitting on a hard old bench'. We'd 'kick up tables, kick-up chairs and ...'

You see, we never considered schooldays as the happiest time of our lives. It was when we were a safe remove from the classroom, and probably had children of our own, that we perpetuated the idea that they were. On reflection, though, they were actually happy.

Think of those long holidays and that is something I admire in the present generation of schoolgoers. They are not content to laze around but are out looking for those few summer jobs to finance their third level education. In our time, there seemed to be less need to get jobs and they were certainly not sought by us.

But I digress. I was about to tell you of those happy days by the sea when young men loved and sometimes lost young women in an age-old courting ritual which appears special for each succeeding generation, but is not.

Then Pat Boone was talking of love letters in the sand and asking his darling to be faithful while he was away, as Mozart had done centuries before in *Cosi Fan Tutte*. Cliff Richard too was doing the singing for us lovelorn youth. That was a time for the summer hops in tennis clubs and local dance halls when the boys stood on one side and girls on the other. The walk across the floor was one of the great acts of male courage and, having reached the other side, words were kept to a minimum. Otherwise, a scriptwriter would have to be employed.

Great opening gambits would be confined to ... 'Do you come here often?' or ... 'I can't dance but I'd love to see you home'. More often than not we went home alone and was it any wonder? We'd boast rather emptily to the lads the next day that we had fallen in love ... again ... and hoped they would not ask any more questions. They might have been golden days but the nights were full of uncertainty for boys trying to be men.

An abiding memory of those times is a tennis club which, like many others, is no more, but was heaven on earth to its members. To put the place in perspective I have to admit that the club little contributed to the advancement of the game locally. Some claimed that the motto was that tennis would be the ruination of the place. It was both apt and prophetic – success was to come later only to herald its closure.

Getting away from it all for an uncertain Leaving Certificate lad was to drop down to the clubhouse on a sunny afternoon, get out those old 78s, forget for a while the Algebraic intangibles and trek with Benny Goodman's 'Caravan' or thrill to Ravel's 'Bolero'.

There were two grass courts of dubious standard, but the main activities of the club were not confined to this area. These were the efforts to chip a golf ball from a tee at the clubhouse doorstep. The sole object of the exercise was to lob the ball to the doorway of the opposition's premises at the other side of the quarry, where the two clubs nestled. We'd play an hilarious game of mixed table tennis with a whole group working their way around the table.

When other clubs closed their doors for the winter then the old club came to life. One show stopper on a Sunday night was 'Girls were Meant to Love and Kiss' from a tenor about whom Tommy O'Brien would have enraptured and consigned to Covent Garden if he had ever been invited to those get-togethers.

Home fixtures were merely tolerated but away matches meant travel, a night out and a laugh, so they were treated with the necessary solemnity. Tennis hops, annual outings too, occupied all for weeks in advance with the going great and the coming back in the nature of a miracle.

The club is no more now and the members scattered but, like the melody, the memory lingers on.

The Kingdom is at Hand

Two mythical Kerrymen met on the road to Dingle some years ago. 'Are you travelling Sunday?' one asked the other.

'I've been thinking about it and I probably will.'

'What would stop you?'

'I don't know, I've never missed a match with that crowd and I suppose, I'm not going to now. It must be the age, or the weather, but I don't feel the same way about travelling these days.'

'I know what you mean ... we've been spoiled with all those wins over the years and now it's hard to summon up the interest.'

'I was thinking the same the other day when reading about their hurlers it's not easy to accept that you won't be winning all the time.'

'My God, you're more than right about that. Time was, it seems like only yesterday, when a defeat was unheard of. Sure there was no one to hold a candle to us.'

'They couldn't lick our boots and I wouldn't admit it, if I was asked, but Cork hurlers were the same.'

'They have no patience where hurling is concerned and we're as bad when we're down in football.'

'I woke bolt upright in the bed the other morning, and the thought struck me that we have seen the best and we'll leave the world and never see their likes again. The wife said that I should see a doctor and shouldn't be getting so upset in the first place.'

'It's all very well, but when your life has been full of dawn trains to Dublin, on golden-mist September mornings, strolling through O'Connell Street, proud as punch, with the colours on the chest and knowing that the lads were all but there, before the ball was thrown in ... they were the times when I blessed my parents for making me a Kerryman.'

'Gan amhras! Sure we hadn't a care in the world and we'd answer to no man.'

'Funny, you're spot on there and I only realised it, when I'd go up for the hurling finals in the late 1970s and see the Corkmen win three in a row; their followers thought 'twould never end too.'

'Of course we didn't win all the time. Ourselves and Cork will remember 1982; they were hooshed out of Croke Park by Kilkenny and we were caught by that sickener of a goal from your man Darby.'

'I'll never forget it as long as I live. I couldn't talk for days ...'twas like the end of the world.'

'And what about the following year? There we were, booking our seats to Dublin and Cork slipped us with that Tadghie Murphy goal in the last second. When I think of all the times we could have won and a kick of a ball robbed us.'

'I agree, but we came back in 1984. And so did Cork hurlers. Sure we sewed up the Centenary Year between us.'

'And well we might. No two counties have given more to the GAA than we have.'

'C'mere we'll have to stop Cork this year, they're getting too cocky altogether. I could feel it when I was up for the Under 21 match last year. There's a fierce buzz about the game in Cork, it reminds me of ourselves when we were flying.'

'Sunday could tell us a lot or nothing at all.'

'Remember the sod will be heavy and we're playing them in their backyard. July, we'll have them in Killarney and they're not going to catch us three years in a row, I can tell you.'

'My God, we'd never live it down.'

Another downpour flecked the horizon as the sun beat a hasty retreat beyond the peninsula. A day was nearly down and the two lads were heading for the first pint.

There wasn't much about the match in the pub, the talk was of the land which had gone under water for the first time in living memory.

It's hard to think of football when you can't find a pitch to play on, was one man's view from a bar stool. The lads agreed and moved off to a corner on their own where they could forget the rain and your man Gorbachev on television.

'So, you'll travel then?'

'Erah, sure you know me, I'm all talk, but when it comes to Sunday morning, the old urge will be there to hit the road.'

'I'll call early for you then, get Mass on Saturday and we'll have one only in Macroom and be in Cork for twelve. We'll park the car and have a few scoops before we head for the Marina.'

'You're a fierce man for planning things, it's only the National League but I'll admit it's beginning to feel like old times just thinking about the journey over the County Bounds. Did you see the team they picked?'

'I did, it'll be fine, we'll be there with a chance and it wouldn't do to show Cork all the cards before July.'

'True for you, now we'll have a pint for the days that are in it ... I love when the hedges get that green sheen on them and the long-acre grass grows longer.'

'You're a bit of a poet, what with everything else. I agree though, we're not dead in Kerry yet, so look out Cork, the Kingdom is at hand.'

SUNDAY IN SEMPLE

The old man sat in the back seat of the gleaming Morris Minor, sandwich and flask cup in his hands; his wife read a Sunday paper in the front passenger seat, there was a Mass on the radio. The ritual had been repeated on a June Sunday since the war years. The children, who would play round the car and climb in and out of the open boot, had grown up and no longer travelled with them but this was another Munster Championship Sunday, life had a pleasant habit of repeating itself.

The couple, as far as I could gather, were from Clare and may have met in Lisdoonvarna on a September night. They shared great loves; their deep faith, their family, a small farm and hurling, not necessarily in that order. They represented the rural heart of Ireland; Gaelic games, which gave the Irish an identity and were born out of a great need, were their recreation – the lighter side of a tough life on the edge of the Burren.

So the trek to Semple continues and the scene described will repeat itself; satellite sophistication beams Sumo wrestling to the living-rooms of Ireland but the passion in the province is still the clash of the ash.

The eve would be make-the-sandwiches time as followers braced themselves for another battle royal.

Of course there are things which have changed over years much as we would have wished for them to remain the same. The cost of a day out with the family is fast becoming prohibitive; travel to the match and entrance to the stadium will soon necessitate a loan and, if the match goer is partial to a 'jouram', then the Credit Union might have to sponsor the weekend.

What is this magnetism, this force which drives the normally calm and unruffled of modern Ireland to march on the cradle of the GAA, sporting banners which proclaim – 'Up the Rebels', 'Come on the Banner'? The real answer is, of course, that the game of hurling is a superb spectacle giving nothing to other national sports and appealing to the Irish man, woman and child as no other.

The experts, former players, readily agree that the game of hurling is now played at an even faster pace than thirty and forty years ago and the participants achieve much greater levels of fitness. Remarkably, it is still essentially amateur with top players receiving no monetary reward for their sacrifices in preparing for a ten month season and meeting the demands of a public who expect the best all the time from their heroes.

There are rewards. The player retains a special place in his own community and with media saturation is a national celebrity. There are the trips to America and the Canaries, but generally the hurler gives more than he receives just to hear the roar of the crowd as he races on to hallowed turf.

I don't know if that couple from Clare still travel, but on Munster Championship days, Thurles can be sure that the square will swarm with colour, the smell of the chips and burger vans and the pre-match excitement which has to be experienced to be understood.

The Morris Minor may be in the breakers' yard, flattened, never to clip along Sunday roads but the heart of the GAA is still in the right place as we face a whole new century.

The mighty Mick Cashman leads the Rockies out of the wilderness – 25 years without a senior county title. He receives the cup from Weeshie Murphy at the Athletic Grounds in 1956

HAND IN HAND WITH DAD

When my father was quite ill, he decided to seek medical advice as to the advisability of attending a Cork and Tipperary match in Limerick. The doctor, a very wise man, thought not, but went on to question him as to how he would put down his day that Sunday. My father described how he would go to early Mass, buy all the papers and read the previews of the match. He would attempt to eat his dinner, as the tension built up before the incomparable Micheál O'Hehir would come on Radio Éireann – Athlone wavelength. The doctor told my father not to dare stay at home as he would be much safer making the journey to Limerick. His view was that listening on radio would be much more likely to exacerbate his condition. The good man was right, and my father strode down the Ennis Road, soaking up the incredible atmosphere of the day and enjoyed the match hugely.

My finest hours were to be with Dad on those golden Sundays. It always seemed a fierce long journey as my heart pounded with the sheer buzz of the whole day. There was the travelling down by car, passing through towns and villages with Mass crowds waving us through, children sitting on gates and garden walls with home-made flags, dolls and teddy bears dressed in red and white.

We'd cross into another county and the colours would be gone and the tension would build up in us even more.

In Limerick we'd get out of the car, stretch our legs, take out the flask and sandwiches (why is a cup of tea always nicer when taken in the open air!). We'd hope to catch a glimpse of the team taxis as we felt part of the extended panel, as it were. The week-nights before we'd have been once, and even twice, to see the training and pick our own teams before they were published on the Wednesday morning in De Paper.

Anyway, back to that walk along the Ennis Road, past those fine houses and then the great moment when we would first glimpse the Limerick

Gaelic grounds spread out to the right of us. I'd break into a trot to get to the turnstiles even though the minor match would not have started. I feared somehow we would not get in. I'd have to wait for Dad and the rest then as they appeared much calmer about it all. Of course, they were not, but they could hide their own excitement better.

Once inside the ground, there would be another rush to get the best spot on the terrace or in the stand if it was not already full. We'd watch the minor match and that is something I miss these days in championship time. The minor game would be a great warm-up to the senior clash, and it's not the same when the same counties are not involved in both matches or there is just a local club game as a curtain-raiser.

Once the 'sliothar' was thrown in the senior game was on, all hell would break loose as both sets of followers roared themselves hoarse. There would not be a quiet moment until half-time then, if we could, we'd sit on the terrace or stand up and stretch if we were in the stand and buy the last of the 'looky lookies' (ice cream). The trick was to be where there was a gathering from the same county; not that there was any great concern about each other and, certainly, there was never need for segregation of the fans, even though the matches always seemed on a knife-edge till the last puck of the ball.

I have two vivid memories of those games in Limerick. One day I became separated from my father and got caught in the crush coming out of the main gates. One portion of the crowd was moving Clare-wards and the other returning to the city and I was caught between the two. I thought my hour had come but had the sense to go with the flow and wait by the side until the big crush was over. I caught up with Dad eventually and his strong warm hand, which he wrapped around mine, was never so welcome, as we moved back to Limerick City.

The other is a golden memory which will always remain with me – on the same Ennis road after a match in which Carrigtwohill's pride and joy, Mattie Fouhy, had excelled. The late Mattie gave me his hurley to keep as we walked down the road with some members of the team still in their togs. Mattie was truly one of the all-time greats and his kindness to me, minutes after the final whistle that day, will never be forgotten.

My hero Mattie Fouhy (Cork) and Sonny Maher (Tipperary) in pursuit of the sliothar as Tony O'Shaughnessy and John Lyons move in support

CURTAIN CALL

It stood at the end of the long narrow hall. It held a glove, the left hand, a golf ball with the rubber bits sticking out and a wrinkled chessie. When we were small we could just tilt the heavy mahogany lid and peek in. The brother kept a Mars bar there for days until it disappeared and I was blamed; the wrapper was found under my bed but 'that meant nothing', I had said bravely, if a little too defensively.

At the front there were two little doors which would open out to reveal ornate lattice wood-work, backed by a canvas-like cloth. To the side, there was a handle which would twist just one way, with each turn, resistance would build, till it would turn no more for small hands.

When it began life, and first came into our house, there was a key for a lock so that the lid could not be lifted. It was, of course, an old gramophone player but when it arrived at our door, it might have been Santa, so great was the welcome for the driver with the docket in his hand.

That signed, he was given a cup of tea and the last slice of apple tart, left over from Sunday tea. That scene stays with me because I never remember another Monday when there was a slice left over. Maybe mother knew the man from the shop would be coming and hid it the night before. Myself and the brother were at home because we had been struck down by that mysterious disease which affects schoolgoers on Mondays to this very day.

It was not always in the hall but had pride of place in the dining-room, next to the old Pye radio. I'm not sure where the old '78' records were stored but there was a marvellous collection of Dad's favourites.

The playing of a record then was something of a ritual, much as tea brewing in China I would think. The record was taken carefully from its paper sleeve, dusted and placed gently on the turntable. Once that wheel was spinning, it was something of an engineering feat to turn over and place the resonator, I think it was known as that, the needle on the outside grooves.

Trembling hands would more often than not drop the needle outside the spinning circle and the handler would be banned for days from going near the machine.

The lid would be kept upright by two metal arms and I recall that one of these broke when forced by a young man standing on a chair so the lid was quite likely to come crashing down, guillotine-like, on the unsuspecting user. For us, it merely added spice to life and the hint of danger made the whole operation particularly fascinating.

I can still see the player, as if it were yesterday, but the records played do not come to mind so easily.

There was, I know, a Bing Crosby record, I think it was 'Don't Fence Me In', and there certainly was 'Cruising Down the River on a Sunday Afternoon' with Prima Scala and his Accordion Band.

My father tried to keep his own personal collection separate from ours, for obvious reasons, and these would have included some beautiful early recordings.

Music was part of our family; not integral, but fringe, so to speak. There'd be the odd musical evenings when my parents would have friends in.

There was always laughter; great waves of laughter coming up through the ceiling to our bedroom above. The brother and myself liked that; you fell asleep easily those nights, secure with all those adults below, behaving not at all like adults as we perceived adults then, but more like ourselves when every second of life was to be enjoyed, not a care in the world. 'In Happy Moments Day by Day' still wafts round the old house conjuring up gentle ghosts of the past.

As we grew a little older we were allowed 'entertain' the guests before we were shunted upstairs. It was, as I recall, something of an ordeal. There was a long room and, thankfully, long curtains at one end. I would give a very soulful rendition of 'On Top of Old Smokey', screened by the curtains, and the brother, a quite competent version of 'North to Alaska', from behind the sofa. I'm not at all sure how all this went down with the visitors and relations but there was general applause and we went to bed, flushed with success.

There were Saturday nights when an uncle would visit and listen with my parents to 'Ballad Makers' Saturday Night'. I remember that they loved Joe Lynch (Dinny to all now) and his rendering of 'Cottage by the Lee'.

Listening to the radio

BRING DOWN THE BLANKETS

When I was a lad I always knew when we were going on holidays because of the heavy blankets. Mum would get one of my taller brothers to take them down from the press in the hall. She'd iron loads of heavy sheets – the ones with the canvas strength to take a month of wear and tear from the lads. This was just after the Second World War so none of your shiny satin variety for a growing family of five boys and one girl.

My mother would iron thousands of clothes too in case we were caught out in the rain and needed a change; it would be August on hols, a wicked month for the sudden shower coming in over the Tower.

The great day of departure was only melodious. The iron bed with the brass knobs would have to be dismantled with much banging and clattering as it was to rest against the wall in the hall. By the time the open pick-up lorry would have arrived the hall and adjoining sitting-room would be piled up with the bed and luggage from big brown suitcases to open cardboard boxes full of food, enough for an army preparing for manoeuvres. If we thought there was loads of stuff in the house then there was even more in the yard and garage. There would be the bikes, big black Rudges and Raleighs, a mattress, pots and pans and the pride of the house, a pressure-cooker which one day exploded on my American aunt and the carrotts, spuds and rack chops shot up into the apple trees in the back. But that's a story for another day's telling, I get ahead of myself.

The row would start with my younger brother as to who would get to travel in the truck with the driver of the lorry; a man who would shift heaven and earth for my Mum and Dad. Compromise was usually the order of the day and if it was fine, one of us would sit in the cab with the driver and the other in the back with the gear, pulling up the heavy tarpaulin if a garda was sighted as things like that did not go down too well with point-duty policemen.

The journey to Ardmore was a holiday in itself. I'm never sure but I

Off to join the bucket and spade brigade

think we went via Midleton, Tallow, by-passing the old be-barrelled bridge at Youghal. This made for a longer journey which was all the better.

The part I hated was when we got to Ardmore and the lorry had to be unloaded. I was never any good at that and would sneak off and search out the pals who lived the year round in the village across the bay.

The rest of the family would arrive in my uncle's car. He was a wonderful kindly man who had cars when few had as he owned a garage. He was generosity itself and on holiday Sunday afternoons he'd ferry us all to lovely goat Island in his Austin Somerset. I can still feel the leather of the seats against the backs of my legs as we children laughed and joked in the back as the two brothers chatted in front, sometimes breaking into a bit of a song – they were grand singers. They'd recall their times at the Father Matthew Hall where uncle appeared in stage productions and Dad trained the hurling team with runs down the Marina. Uncle would recall John McCormack singing in Cork and those were the times I wished would never end.

The car would stop at the uncle's bungalow and we'd tear down the stony road and leap into the meadow field which brought us down to the cliff top above the beach and caves. We'd tog off by the rocks at the opening to a cave and charge into the sea which always seemed to have thunderous waves. Then we'd play a soccer match with our cousins and summer friends and cool off in the end with another swim.

It would be back up the hill to be met at the corner with the aroma of a big fry wafting from the bungalow. Mum and Auntie would have gone up earlier and we'd sit down to a grand feed.

Uncle would drive us back to the village in time for evening devotions in the church by the sea. I can still hear *Tantum Ergo* as we sat centre aisle where we filled a seat between us. After Benediction, we'd play release outside the church while the adults stood and talked about whatever. It would be late evening when we'd fall into bed; tired but looking forward to the next day of our holidays.

SUN AND MIST OF OUR SALAD DAYS

I can still feel the wet sand between the Franciscan sandals and the soles of my feet. We'd sit huddled to the shelter side of the fishing boat which lay on the strand between tides.

Every few minutes my father's head would dip and look out from under the plastic macks and peer at the sky. 'It's clearing from Youghal, it'll be fine in a minute', he'd tell the little group whose game of hurling had been halted for the umpteenth time. The man would never accept that there would be anything that would remotely diminish the enjoyment of his precious few weeks away from a job into which he put so much for forty-nine weeks of every one of fifty years.

Such thoughts cross what passes for my mind as I contemplate the arrival of summer – you know, the long weekend between spring and autumn.

Those summers of my childhood and youth appear now to have had a greater intensity about them; their joys were more compressed into four short weeks of August when we rented a house for something like £20 for the entire month. It was, of course, my father's holiday, my mother was content to ensure that his time was clutter-free. They'd go for long walks around the hill behind the house and along the road to Youghal and Whiting Bay.

It was a carefree time but my father never shed the sense of discipline which he developed in the job. It threw inevitable burdens on the rest of the house. That marvellous lady who never complained would have produced a large breakfast for the whole household which, counting summer friends, could number fourteen. She'd then have prepared a cauldron of new potatoes, vegetables and meat before we'd struggle out of our beds to the father's tune that we had missed the best part of the day. They were truly salad days in that their pleasures can still be recalled and savoured by those who lived them but, on reflection, this far removed, my mother and the mothers of the 1940s and 1950s, are surely sainted for their unselfishness.

I can still smell the evenings. After tea we youngsters would be allowed walk the beach to the village across the bay. It's interesting now to remember that we'd leave with the father's admonitions; 'don't forget to call into the church first and be home before nine o'clock'. That freedom of striding down the stony Curragh Road, sharing a Woodbine which we'd hidden under a rock in the ditch the night before, was the high point of the day. No human pleasure is without some uncertainty and we'd be careful to stub the butt before we'd reach the track behind the strand as the great man's figure would be standing at the same porch-door, fields away. As the last curl of smoke would waft from the pocket of the pants, we'd turn and wave, not without a tinge of remorse at our poor deceit.

The attraction of the evening was, of course, meeting the girls. We'd never admit it, even to ourselves, but the sitting on the storm-wall or leaning over the rail above the pier under the cliff, was a kind of a mating ritual of incredible innocence but no less pleasurable for that. As we moved through the village we'd meet pairs of parents, watchful, but understanding. With what we considered an incredible sense of timing, we would ensure that the girls were never in our company when a parent would come into sight. We'd be parents ourselves before we'd realise that nothing really happened in our lives that our guardians were not fully aware of and had discussed when young heads had fallen sound asleep.

There were low points too. The rain clouds would swirl in over the tower and the mist would be down for days. The boredom would be relieved by counting the number of nuns who would venture along the strand. It was amazing how the pre-television generation could occupy themselves.

Obedience was very high on my father's list of virtues. There was one evening when we had been told to go home early because we had been noisy in the main street. We were halfway across the strand when the mackerel broke a few yards from us as we paddled along, shoes in hand. We were in the middle of them like a flash, up to our waist in sprat whose silver bellies sparkled against the dark green backs of the marauding mackerel. The fish that evening drove up on the beach, stranded by a retreating wave. We forgot everything in the excitement and did not spot my father striding towards us. There was a roar, the cousin and myself, soaked to the skin, ran for our lives. We were in bed when he reached the house and it took the divine intervention of my mother to save us. I sometimes roar at my own children and have been disappointed at their response. Does anything really change?

Postscript: Over forty years later I found an old diary of Dad's a page of which had written on it: 'Paid Ardmore grocery bill today'. It had a December date and I thought to myself of how much we took for granted those salad days of carefree fun and games as the parents of the time made so many sacrifices.

One sunlit day in the summer of long ago

RIVERDANCE — 1950s STYLE

In our time we were no riverdancers – at least I wasn't. I had difficulty sorting out my left from my right, without taking the higher maths of quick ... quick ... slow. Fred Astaire and Ginger Rogers had my undivided attention on the silver screen and once, when I tried the old three steps of a stairway at one go, I ended on the flat of my back, lying on my ego.

We waltzed around the crystal-glazed floors of summer haunts and winter ballrooms of romance. As with most things in life, the anticipation is a finer thing than the realisation. I remember particularly the getting ready for nights at the local hop, when the height of our excitement would be to share a mineral with the girl most fancied at the time. We, the lads would never admit it, but we spent as much time as the girls sprucing ourselves for the night ahead.

I thought I was the bees' knees with my big shirt collar outside the sports coat; my hair-oiled head plastered down in the tonsorial style of the time. I'm talking about the 1950s, when there was a great sea-change coming over Ireland and I was intent on being a dedicated follower of fashion.

The shoes would be polished, and polished again, with a spit on the cloth so that I could see myself in the shiny leather. I remember sneaking out my father's patent leather shoes one night when on holidays. Wouldn't you just know there would be a problem. The dance went a bomb and myself and my friend walked home two of the girls from the dance. It was one of those balmy nights without a puff of wind but overcast. We reached their home and chatted about the fun of that night. We happy four promised to meet again the next day. As we lads turned to walk down the road I realised I had stepped into a little stream which crossed over from the boreen by the side of the house. The shoes were soaked and I had to walk home in my bare feet. Next morning I heard my Dad's voice in the kitchen. He was asking mother about his shoes. Then I remembered. I had left them on the still warm plate of the oil stove the night before. The leather had cracked like the base of a dried-out desert pond. I avoided Dad that day as some things are best left unsaid.

The happiest thought I have of that time when the summers seemed to drift sweetly from tennis hops to holiday halls, would be for the girl who guided my untrained feet along the shiny boards. I learned from this brave soul the intricacies of the old time waltz, the fox-trot and even the tango.

It was a strange new freedom to be able to walk across, if not exactly glide across a floor, without falling over myself. It was like playing the guitar without looking down, not to have to count how many feet I had and not wonder why they always moved at the same time. I stood on many a pretty toe and put a large heel on the back of many a passing ankle before I managed to get round without missing the turn and ending up in someone's lap.

It took a while to master the art but at least I was now less of a danger to the other floor users. I could take off the L-Plates and make like I was years moving around the dance-halls of my well-spent youth.

On the road again – Dixies on tour

OVER THE COUNTY BOUNDS

The air was heavy with exhaust fumes; it was one of those hot, thundery, July Sundays and the traffic was tailed back to Ballyvourney as the County Bounds were negotiated. It must have been a good few years ago, when cars were more prone to overheating, as a good few bonnets were up. The primus kettles for the picnic before the match were being put to good use.

There was a fair bit of to'ing and fro'ing to a nearby stream, with a few bored sheep chewing away, looking up just now and then to see what was all the fuss about. The snarl sorted itself out and we made it to the game in Killarney without further mishap. They have improved cars and re-aligned the County Bounds, so that scene is one for the archives only.

Strange, isn't it, I can remember that and I can't remember the match itself. You could say, and I know you wouldn't, that it was because there were few enough games to remember for Cork followers down the years. There could be some disputing that, but admittedly, the good days in the Kingdom have been fairly sparse for the reds, with a few notable exceptions.

Funny too, but I would prefer to travel to Kerry than see the finals in Cork. That is not to be unfaithful to the home county, but there is that special attraction of showdowns in Killarney, which lift them out of the mere milieu of sport, onto an infinitely higher plain of a social experience.

Once the eldest son and myself took our tent to 'Heaven's Reflex' and had the time of our lives. It was around the time when Cork were beginning to wrest the crown from the Kings of Gaelic Football. The atmosphere on that Saturday night in Killarney was electric as the trainloads of Rebels began to arrive. There wasn't a pub with an empty stool and there was a carnival atmosphere in the streets.

I can remember a knot of tourists looking on in quiet amazement at the scenes; they must have been wondering how so many could have so much fun.

Strange too that it was on that weekend more than any other that I felt closest to my son. We have no idea when that happens in a lifetime; the secret is to relish the time when it does.

All smiles for the camera!

A FAMOUS VICTORY RECALLED

Mist rested round ragged fields of Sliabh Luachra. Sounds of tyre rubber on wet-black roads, strident car horns piercing country calm. Sunday at seven. Kerry were beaten but the county absorbed it all with the dignity and calm of a ruler.

Corkmen shook themselves and reminded each other they were in power, uncertain of their feelings in an uncertain year; six Sundays on county roads, Killarney twice, despair, then ecstasy.

Red and white lit up the sombre grey of the evening and the pubs on the road home filled, a time for a quiet pint and reflection, the occasional shout of triumph, but generally, respect for the bereaved and an unspoken prayer for the well-being of the survivors.

... and the cars trundled on, out of the highways and by-ways, a line of grass down centre-road, giving new meaning to the term 'dual carriageway'; County Kerry knows too the reality of being 200 miles from the pale of power.

They tell me that people in that area live longer there than anywhere else and I'm not at all surprised. There is a longevity and timelessness about the place, a stillness cocooning the people from the trauma known to city dwellers who sometimes live as if there was no today to be enjoyed and only tomorrow to be feared.

Kerry people are generous but then Kerry followers have known such happiness that the occasional tear merely clears the ducts. There is tangible mutual respect between Cork and Kerry sportsmen but the acceptance of the rebels as a continuing football force could yet prove to be hard to bear for broad shoulders in Ciarraí.

It has all been said; a Kerry team who surely, at its peak, was the greatest of all time. I know it is an extravagant claim and there are people alive who have seen brilliant performers but, for sustained greatness, that Kerry side

Aerial combat – Cork's Coleman Corrigan and Kerry's Eoin Liston in full flight as Jack O'Shea swoops in for the breaking ball

could have no equals and we have been privileged to see them in action. That Galway team of the 1960s was a superb outfit, ahead of its time but, you heard one of their own, Enda Colleran, say that we have seen the end of the best.

What of Cork? I know a genuine follower who would offer three All-Ireland Hurling medals for one Football if they were his to give. This man is not usually given to such extravagance but it does under-score the poverty which Cork Football had endured as the Hurlers strung success like a daisy chain. Billy Morgan's men established themselves as true champions and the stamp of public approval came with that victory in Killarney where many a good Cork side had faltered down through the years.

Teddy McCarthy in command over Ambrose O'Donovan, as Larry Tompkins awaits the outcome

SOMETHING WENT SPOOK IN THE NIGHT

We all have moments in our lives when we are scared; not your common-or-garden frightened, but really nervous about something stiffening the neck-hairs and making palms clammy but cold. I suppose around Halloween it is understandable, things going spook in the night, occupying fertile minds.

I have one particular experience which gives a jolt whenever it comes to mind. Strangely enough, it has nothing to do with the time of the year, but happened on a starry August night when I was very young and very impressionable. I suppose the only thing different now is that I'm older.

Anyway, about that night, and the moment when I thought my end had come. I was with a few pals and had called one evening to an old holiday friend of the family who, to my mind, was the best story-teller I have ever known.

We'd sit on the stone floor of the kitchen and he'd reel off from his high backed, wooden chair marvellous accounts of pirates and smugglers along the coast, long before his time, but told with the essential sense of witness.

The big open fire would flick shadows round the big room and the more we'd listen the more he'd embellish. We were transported round the world without ever leaving his kitchen.

He is long since gone to his reward but I will never forget how much he opened our young minds to that mysterious world of adventure and tales of the unexpected.

We'd leave his cottage with the heightened sense of there being more to this world than met the eye. We'd pass an old disused quarry and we'd imagine that was where the boundary of the high seas would be found a century before. Beneath us, on the cliff road, the crashing waves would stir up thoughts of silently oared boats slipping into dark coves, the big ship at anchor outside the submerged line of rocks.

On the way home, further up the road, there was an ancient grave site, more a burial mound which, even in daylight, I moved past at speed. That particular night the chatter was nervous and I was not at all sure if it was better to walk in front of, or behind, my companions. No one admitted to it but we were all edgy and would break into a gallop at the slightest sound.

We rounded a corner of the road home to the village and had relaxed somewhat as the oil lamps and Tilley lights beckoned from small windows in the distance.

Then we saw it. There was a shadowy figure against the skyline.

You will have gathered that I'm not the bravest heart. I stood clung to the rough stone road; unable to go back and incapable of putting one foot in front of the other.

Even the brave ones were not all that certain about the next move. The figure just stayed there on top of the ditch and not a stir out of it.

I had decided my hour had come and, in very adult fashion, was making my peace with my Maker. One of the bigger lads said we'd make a run for it, but I was rooted to the spot. I had to be lifted bodily and the mad rush down the road began.

To my horror we were running, or rather, I was being carried toward the figure, I decided the bravest thing to do was to close my eyes and hope that if it came down on to the road my end would be quick and painless.

The next thing I remember I was back on my feet and they were actually working, my feet that is. I did not stop running until we were in the main street, unlit then, but with comforting, occupied houses on either side.

The older ones made light of the incident and said that they never had any doubt that they would be more than a match for the threatening creature a mile back the road.

It was about a week later that I found myself in the area, speeding by in the safety of the back seat of my uncle's car. As we passed, I stole a glance at the spot where we had seen it. There it was .... a white-thorn bush!

Radio days

Radio was a focal point in the house. In Brian Friel's *Dancing at Lughnasa* the writer, through a narrator on stage, gives a glimpse of the way we were, or, rather the way it seemed to be, in a fairly typical rural household of the 1930s. Now I was not exactly alert in the 1930s, but things did not change all that much in the 1940s and 1950s, so those of my generation who have seen the play, will agree that the Donegal playwright is very accurate in his evocation of not so much the time but the atmosphere.

It is true that our ability to recall is limited by the memory's happy knack of blocking out the reality as it were. We remember best that which gave us most pleasure at the time. Much in the same way all summers of the past were golden and never ending. But, of course, they were not and they did ... end.

Now, through the many sacrifices of our parents, my pals and myself would spend part of the summer in Ardmore. Substitute the place where you were most happy as a child and read on.

Anyway, in the play one of the 'Mundy' daughters has been shopping in the town and brings back with her an old recharged wet-cell battery for the radio. I could identify with that scene. I can remember waiting for the bus one Saturday as my Dad would be bringing down the battery from Cork. The bus would have stopped at the old Youghal Bridge with goods and passengers having to move across the span of the Blackwater estuary as the bridge had barrels every few yards to deter heavy vehicle traffic. Then another bus would be waiting on the other side. As I say, we think now that every day was sunny then, but, more often than not, there would be a fierce wind and driving rain so the trip was something of a marathon.

That afternoon the rejuvenated radio would sparkle to life on the big kitchen table and I'd be indoors catching every word on the cricket tests. Yes, there I was reared on GAA affairs but fascinated about the happenings at

The Oval, Headingly and Lords. I hadn't an idea where those exotic places were but when John Arlott would talk about the gas-works end I could see the bowler thundering up to the crease.

Sure with an imagination like that I had no need of television but it would come in the 1960s and nothing would ever be the same again. That healthy sense of mystery and dramatic distance would be lost and we'd become a know-it-all, nothing surprises, generation.

Have you noticed how the radios now are all buttons and mysterious tuning systems which only a ten-year-old reared on computers could handle. One of my lads has programmed the car radio and every press of the button has been deeper into the rap music jungle. God be with the days when we'd turn the old dial and find ourselves in touch with Allouis (never found out where that was), Hilversum, AFN and Moscow (well it was on the dial even if I never quite made contact with the boys in the Kremlin).

On a quiet night, when study was not going too well (and that was often!) you could move to another band and listen to the 'dot, dot, dash' of shipping around the world. Best of all was the quite wonderful sound from those radios which, despite the incredible advance of technology, has not, in my view, been matched for sheer aural sweetness.

Hilversum calling

THE ROAD TO NOWHERE

There is a road which now leads to nowhere. Once it led the traveller from a busy fishing and farming community to the main road and on to the nearest town. The hungry sea has left that little road hanging some thirty feet above the beach and a sign says simply ... No Road.

Some twenty yards back lies the ruins of a long low cottage, now derelict with a slate roof which had replaced the thatch, holed and open to the elements. I felt a great sense of another time; a feeling too, that I was trespassing on the lives of those who were gone. They had lived full lives without thought that one Sunday afternoon another would pass and find toppled stone, choking briar, flapping corrugated sheets, where once windows caught the morning sunshine of days full of golden promise.

I suppose I am particularly conscious of the scene because I knew those who had been there; those who had known bitter winters when the southwesterlies whipped across the bay and sent the sea biting at the clay cliff and foundations of the causeway road which is now only marked by seaweed covered stone and the arched remains of a short rise bridge.

Nearby lies a low line of rocks where Carrigeen moss was gathered in late August, dried in the short sun bursts and bagged in old pillow slips and stored for the winter in a hot press. Its curative powers were legendary and one mother swore that it was a match for all ills.

I never stayed in that cottage but heard many stories which gave me a feel for the time and place.

Days were spent trekking the few fields to a little cove which has great dark weeping caves. As children we were told that one led underground to another house in the lea of a hill, a half mile away. I've never had the courage since to travel into that cave and disprove the tale.

Some early mornings in the cottage by the cliff were special I'm told. They'd be in August when the overnight dew would moisten the warm earth and mushrooms could be found along the cliff fields where animals had been tethered. Apparently the smell of the frying pan would rouse an entire household quicker than all the shouts of 'get up'.

Weekends were special too as those who were back at work would bring down fresh supplies with shop cakes, a particular target for the young holidaymakers. The radio would be the only contact with the outside world; not that there could be anything as important as the happenings round and about the little household.

Some years later I stayed as a child in the area and our delight was going up the stony road to the farm where we'd get the milk in a can. I still recall one particular disaster when one of the gang boasted that he could swing the can round without spilling a drop. The handle came loose and there was black tea for all that night and a sore behind for one circus performer.

At the farm we'd be allowed to slide in the hay in the barn and one of the farmer's family would hide English threepenny bits and we'd spend hours searching for them. Remarkable the simple joys which could occupy us in those days.

Corn cutting was magic too. I'd get the job with the farmer's eldest daughter of bringing out the tea, sandwiches and curranty cake to those in the fields.

The baskets would be placed on the dray, the sides of which had been removed and we children would take turns in guiding the horse along the narrow lane and across the fields, already stuked, to the last field overlooking the sea which was always the first to ripen but strangely, the last to be cut. The tea poured and the sandwiches taken out of their linen cloth cover, there'd be man's talk of tomorrow's weather, the trouble with the reaper and binder and the need to get more baling twine in the town the next morning. The tea in those mugs has never tasted as well since we youngsters were blessed to be part of a way of life that would be gone when the first combine harvester trundled into the farmyard. Machines would take the drudgery out of farming but they'd bag the magic too.

Ballrooms of romance

The poster said Dickie Rock was coming to town. It reminded me of the time when we'd spend hours 'dolling' ourselves up for a night at the Arc, Majorca or Redbarn. Did we think they'd ever end? The Arc in Cork was a particularly favourite haunt of mine when the Brilliantine would leave a tide mark just around the neck where the mother's carefully ironed shirt collar met skin.

We thought we were marvellous and we only had to stride across the floor and the girls would be ours. That we couldn't dance or even walk properly did not concern us; John Travolta was still in nappies and we were, in our view, the answer to every maiden's prayer. That we were otherwise, awkward gangling youths enjoying our first taste of freedom from parental control had not quite sunk it.

They were ballrooms of romance; winter palaces when a nod was as good as a wink to the right girl. Or so we thought. The nod was usually the poor girl's effort to avoid our leers across the floor and the wink was more likely dust in their pretty eyes.

There was always a terrific build-up in the Arc before the main band came on the balcony style stage. For me, it all began with the Clipper Carlton; for others the Royal Showband were heaven and the Dixies would be up there with the best in no time at all. All were great and we did not know it then but this was the beginning of a rich cabaret-style period in live entertainment which has never been surpassed. The open air concert was confined to public parks and regattas and the thought that whole stadia would be filled for Bono and Jacko would be then in the realm of science fiction. Woodstock, flower-power were still a decade away.

There was a real buzz too, about a night at Majorca, Dickie ruled and one whip of those slim hips sent tremors of excitement through the females and decided the males to practise a bit more in front of the mirror when they got home. Not that dance steps were all that necessary as rock and roll was king and the flick of a wrist and odd shuffle of the blue suede shoes would get you through the night. I knew of no band which gave more sustained performance over two and a half hours as the Capitol. One balmy summer's night in Redbarn they belted out the numbers for fully three hours. It did all come to an end with the odd flicker of revival which served only to remind us of the excitement and relative innocence of lost youth.

One October day in 1964 I saw a poster, in a Galway hotel, announcing the arrival that night of the Clippers. It was a chance to relive the happy hours. It was not to be. A few people turned up, and to their credit those professional musicians from over the border played out their entire show.

It would be years later that I would meet up with The Clippers in Jury's Hotel, Cork cabaret. Again the fans did not throng the place, but there were tablefuls of the faithful. Time can be very cruel on all our fond memories.

Down the Arc

Up for the match

There is that almost intangible sense of a year on the wind-down. Chestnut leaves have gone brown and brittle at the edges; there is a crispness in the air with just a hint – a smidgen – of frost as the warming sun burns off the necklace dew mantled on the fields – autumn's gossamer calling-card presaging a change of seasons, a respite before the short days ahead.

Indian summers they still call these bonus days of warm streets and great splashes of light.

The children are safely back at school and traffic is heavier in the mornings, so it must be that time of year when sport takes advantage of firm sod to complete the annual ritual of separating the winner from the runner-up.

Soon the champions will be known and those who lose will, sadly, be just a statistic in the right-hand margin of the handbook, forgotten even as a two-marker in a pub quiz.

I will never forget seeing my first All-Ireland in Dublin. No, that is not quite true as the game, though it was Wexford and Cork in a titanic struggle, has not emblazoned itself on the memory. Yet I will forever recall that wonderful weekend.

Remember a trip to Dublin then was something out of the ordinary even for a teenager. Adults and important people went to Dublin but youngsters knew their place which was at home, glued to the wireless and hanging on every word from Micheál O'Hehir. Anyway, we reached Dublin about six o'clock on the Saturday evening and, to be honest, it seemed then that the capital was on the other side of the world. The road from Cork to Dublin was a corkscrew affair in comparison to nowadays and dual carriageways were something the Germans had but had not yet reached the drawing board here.

There we were, up from Cork and, real posh, staying at the Clarence for the weekend. God, the thrill of it. To have your bags taken to the room; to look out the large windows at the Liffey flowing by. There was time for high tea with iced buns and cheese cakes.

Dad had secured tickets for us for the Theatre Royal on the Saturday night. Now there are those of you who will be saying what was so great about that? Well, I'll tell you the programme then. It was a short feature, usually a comedy, a full variety stage show, with the high-stepping Royalettes and guest stars, and, then the feature film, which I can remember to this day was *Tiger Bay*.

By the time we reached the street outside it was after 11 and it was time to walk back along the quay where the hotel porter met us at the door and inquired if we had had a nice evening. I did not want to go to bed that night for fear the magic spell would be broken.

Breakfast the next morning was something else. I wanted everything on the menu and seemed to get it. Great half-grapefruits topped with brown sugar squirted juice all over the place when poked with a big spoon. Now porridge at home was no big deal but I had two helpings that morning because it was being served up to me and had a dollop of cream on top – the luxury of it all.

That morning we walked over to the Phoenix Park and Aras an Uachtarán could have been the White House as it glistened in the sun. It was great to listen to the adults talking about the game and being part of a world which was just opening up to me and would give me so much fun down all the years.

When I bring my own children to matches now I wonder will they have the same fond memories.

BEING THERE IS ALL THAT MATTERS

The nice lady in the shop totted up on the back of a brown paper bag: 'That'll be £1.56,' she told the Corkman who had forgotten to buy something for the kids in Dublin. It was Monday, high afternoon in Abbeyleix, the first Monday after All-Ireland Sunday.

Down the street in Morrissey's the woman from Washington was observing a ritual not mentioned in her guide book, but, nevertheless, quaint, to her trans-Atlantic way of thinking.

The man in the red and white cap, who hated draws, sipped his Carling and showed no emotion when the camera flash splashed back from the high shelves of bottles and sweet jars. The picture would be in the album by Christmas; something to show the grandchildren in Tacoma Park, DC.

Her husband sat in the corner and sipped a glass of Guinness. He was not usually confused; he had built his fortune on the premise that Mondays were sacred, that work was the only ethic, and, here he was, soaking up the brewed charm of a country which takes Mondays off because matches are played on Sundays.

His wife had reached the glass cabinet, which displayed the shop assistants' list, dating back to the last century. How quaint, she thought. Good management, thought her husband. Another Corkman was reminded of great teams of the past. All life is in the eye of the beholder.

There were cheers from the snug in the back. There was an action-replay of the match.

Dublin, on the day before, was particularly well behaved; it had a somewhat jaded but welcoming face. The tourists must have felt all the colours, green, gold and red, were the pageantry of the fair lady's birthday but the boyos of Meath and the headbanders of Cork had other things on their minds.

The Hill 16 pub in Gardiner Street stood proud as the Alamo; a welcome watering hole surrounded by inner-city decay. A well-kept street corner park contrasted with the slums which overlooked its manicured grass and shrubberies.

New red brick fascia houses had stemmed, if not stopped, the eye-sore civic neglect. We were only a few hundred yards from the foremost street in Ireland and heavy chains, attached to steering wheels, remind us all of our vulnerability.

The crack in the pub was mighty, not a cross word between opposing fans; Barney Rock scored a goal on the screen in some past match and the local clientele roared their delight – Ireland, Sunday, High Noon.

The touts around the ground got their come-uppence. They could not give away Canal and Hill 16 tickets and they must have been tempted to do the unheard of; attend the match themselves, a sort of busman's holiday.

Along the narrow lanes, past neat houses in the shadow of the then ugly stand bearing the name of a great Gael. Up the stone steps to the blast of sound as Kerry minors rock the Dubs with a goal.

A ribbon of red slip-streams from the narrow passage and the Canal End is awash with flags; it would appear to the one-match must-be-seen-there corporate ticket brigade that there are interesting American, Canadian, Russian, Japanese and Turkish influences in the Rebel Army. Meath roar out and Hill 16 is alive with plainsmen, the green and gold flutters as proudly as on Tara's Hill.

Tension chokes the committed and the game is enjoyed best by the neutrals, but they too are sucked into the Hurricane Gilbert-force second half.

Crowds converge at the Canal End afterwards and some fans walk on water, it seems, to the safety of the far bank. To think it must all be gone through again is not easy to accept but the printing press rolls, letters of application must be written; being there is all that matters.

(Postscript: We know now that Cork lost the replay with Meath but would take Mayo in 1989 and settle a score with Meath in 1990 as the second leg of a double).

DOUBLE VISION

They said it would never be done. No county would ever win two senior (hurling and football) All Irelands in a season. In 1990 Cork took the first step in beating a gallant Galway in the hurling final. It really was a splendid day out with the fabulous atmosphere on the streets. There was not a cross word between the fans and Dublin had a carnival air about it.

On the night before, I was up in Kingscourt, Co. Cavan, which nestles in that lovely Dún an Rí wooded estate. I learned a new meaning of the expression 'only an hour from Dublin', Navan that is. On our way to the match we just slipped in and out of An Uaimh, worked our way left along a secondary road to the main road which sweeps through Ashbourne and on then through Finglas, past Glasnevin.

I tell you this because it was an interesting experience to go to Croke Park on the day of the All-Ireland Hurling Final through counties like Cavan and Meath who are not associated with the code, more with the bigger ball.

It was only when we parked the car in a quiet suburban estate, off St Adolphus road, that the adrenaline started to flow. The sun, despite the forecast, positively beamed down and all round the car boots were open and the flasks and sandwiches rested on hot car roofs.

In sight of Croke Park and standing on a canal bridge, with the gable end of the Hogan Stand in the distance, I thought to myself, 'may there always be All-Ireland final days, September Sundays, the banter of fans anticipating the match, the hats and colours men, the self-appointed parkers with their peak caps and Sunday paper in the pocket'.

They pay writers millions in Hollywood for such incredible scripts:
McCarthy Cup
Act One: Enter Cork hurlers, written out and written off.

Act Two: Exit Cork hurlers, champions.

Interval: Two weeks, drinks at the bar for the fans to discuss the next performance.

O'Connell Street on the morning of the Football Final could have been Barracka or Shandona; there were Cork people, ticket touts, and more Cork people. I wondered had everyone come up for the match, or, had the rest of the country decided that this was going to be the day when the real Republic would cede from the rest of the island and they wanted to be on a winner.

Up, and just beyond the Garden of Remembrance, two end-of-season tourists sat on church steps, bewitched, bothered and bewildered by it all. They had heard no doubt that Dublin could be heaven with coffee at eleven, but this wasn't even Stephen's Green, according to their maps. Their gentle query as to what was happening, would have been met with ... 'match boy ... match girl!' as the river of red and white bubbled merrily by. Heading towards the Canal, with the cries of 'buying or selling' ringing in their ears and that particular aroma of burger meat frying on griddles, the nearest many of us will ever get to 'Sunday morning coming down' in old New York.

In, and around, the Hill 16 pub, the Dub and Cork fans were talking tactics; an interesting alliance. Already the great movement of people pushed along the approach streets to Croke Park and for the first time the reds and greens coalesced at the ticket-check barriers. There was no rancour, no animosity and there would be none later when it was all over. Successive years of fierce competition had somehow engendered a deepening respect between the Canal and Hillsiders. Inside you could bottle the tension and it wasn't half-time in the minor match. The League of Nations were in particularly lively mood to the right, hailing every Kerry score with unabashed bias; the county bounds had somehow crumbled and it was Munster against the rest of the world.

Cork erupted from the tunnel at the Canal end, made for the bench and faced more shots from the cameramen than they would for the rest of the afternoon; we were not to know that then.

Sam Maguire

Act One: Enter the Holders Cork and centre stage favourites, Meath

Act Two: Hail, The Rebels are Champions and Cork has the Double.

The match you have read about, and, this far removed, I'm not going to rewrite it for you. Now children can tell their children that they held the hands of their mums and dads when Cork brought home the double in September 1990.

Cork became the centre of the sporting universe; well, for Cork people anyway. As the open double-decker bus moved past St Patrick's Church one man told his son that the likes would not be seen again – Irish sporting history had been made.

McCarthy and Maguire had come home.

The Rebels round Barry's Corner

THE LIGHT OF OTHER AUTUMN DAYS

The back lawn, never likely to make *Homes and Gardens,* has the texture of a Madras cricket crease. Soon however, the rainy season will have arrived, then the slate on the roof meant to be replaced last March, and the window which was not opened for years, might move up the list of jobs to put off until they really had to be done.

There is something special about a sunny autumn day. It's as if you had curled up for the winter and found that the summer continues to roll on. You don't do much with those bonus days but it is nice to know they are still around.

Two activities which always gave the utmost pleasure was searching for wild mushrooms and picking blackberries. I knew some great fields for mushrooms in my youth, but fertiliser and progress put paid to them. I always hated getting up early in the mornings but, once the word was out that conditions were right, I'd be out, my shoes tracing dewy patterns on the grass.

When you found one, you usually found a circle of them, if someone had not got there before you. People like to fish, walk a bank of a river or lie in the sun, my idea of relaxation is roaming through fields while on the trail of the mighty mushroom. I suppose we'll reach a stage when the wild mushroom will have died out altogether. Its disappearance will not make page one but it will be a measure of disregard for nature's gifts to man.

Now picking 'blackas' remains special for me and I'm sure for a lot of you. I knew a winding lane which I always felt went on for ever. On either side, in those days, the brambles almost blocked out the sky as the only real traffic would have been the open drays bringing in the harvest straw which would snag on wild thorn branches.

The best of the crop would always be at the top, so parents were allowed come along for that purpose. By evening time, we children would be a

Picking 'blackas'

pleasant shade of purple in face, arms and hands. There would be fierce rivalry as to who had picked the most and disappointment when mother would have poured the lot into one container for the journey home.

It's the 'chessie' season too and I notice in my contacts with the real world, children, that conkers are very much back. In my house, they are under the piano – the chessies, not the children – in the fire-hearth and underneath beds. At present my youngest is doing very well with a chestnut which looks so shrivelled and hard that it must have been last year's crop or one of mine from the dark ages!

When we were young we had all sorts of ways of hardening them for battle. Even the string used be dipped in something to strengthen it. Many a tear was shed when a particularly good conker had fought its last fight and lay in pieces on the footpath. We'd bury it in the garden, with due ceremony, in the hope that it would reseed and grow into a famous tree. We'd be waiting!

There is a little ribbon of wood near where I grew up, still standing and giving pleasure to those who stroll through its shaded walk. Many years ago it was the scene of great adventures when you were either an American Indian or trigger happy Cowboy. That we all survived those slap-happy days, falling from overhanging branches into muddy pools of water is a wonder to me now.

Do you remember when the footpaths were littered with youngsters playing glassie-alleys – all right, marbles? The more marbles you could accumulate, particularly the giant 'blood' coloured ones, which could be bought in Woolies, the greater was your standing in the community.

Can you recall when we beat a little piece of wood round the roads of our youth? They were those colourful, little barrel-tops and the slimmer, striped 'racers', whipped along by a cord on a stick. You'd be doing fine until someone playing hoops, the old bicycle wheel rim, beaten, or guided along, would come crashing through.

You had to be careful, too, that you didn't disrupt a preliminary world championship round of pickey (hop scotch). Anyway, the girls, and sometimes the lads, would draw out a set of boxes and you got on one leg and flicked with the side of your shoe a little stone, or even the lid of a boot-polish tin, taking care not to go outside the boxes or land the pick on the line.

Back to conkers, I can now reveal that I stayed on top of my profession by developing the twitching wrist technique which ensured my chestnut was always moving when the other fellow struck. Devious but effective.

They came from other streets to observe the performance and just when I was about to retire the all-conquering conker and have it mounted, a lad from the village smashed his way to victory and the title was gone – they never come back.

Ring-a-ring-a-rosie in a school yard

THE FOOTBALLER

A little street disappeared and the winter before it became a blank wall, I had the delightful experience of meeting 'Mighty Mouse'. He stood, inches high, in the bitter cold darkness of the morning looking up to the top floor of the house which had more windows shuttered than curtained.

'Mister, knock on the door, will ya?' he asked, school bag propped between frozen feet, hands cupped before his face. He expected me to oblige, so I did.

'The footballer?' I inquired, as I had seen another half-pint doing a Kevin Keegan (remember him) around city car parks in the evening dusk.

'He's not the footballer,' with considerable indignation my young friend retorted, 'I'd murder him in a match any day'.

There was no sign of the pal so I made to move on.

'Mister, give another bang, he's half deaf that fellah is.'

Another pull at the old rusting knocker and little twinkle toes was about to appear. Tiny hands pulled from inside and his young buddy helpfully kicked the door open.

'Who's your man?' he asked.

'Him, he's all right, "twas him what banged on the door.'

From that point I was ignored.

'Have you your "ecker" done?'

'My mother did mine, mothers are great ... sometimes.'

'Did you bring your togs? We've a match against Sully's Quay.'

'Naw, I'm giving up football. I wants to be a detective.'

With that they rounded the corner and I never saw them together again. I saw the ball wizard many times after, playing the rest of the world from foot paths to road to the accompaniment of shrieking brakes and horn blasts. It was heady stuff, scuffed shoes and socks round the ankles. He must have changed his mind about becoming a detective.

They both became children of suburbia and the old houses were pulled down.

Their spirits jink and feint where shining new shop fronts mask the way we were.

Sunny smile on a cloudy day in Ardmore

THE SHOPKEEPER

There is a universality about the small shopkeeper. I have particularly fond memories of a lady (my aunt in Blackrock) long gone to the big store in the sky. Remember the first time you placed grubby hands on a counter top and asked for a penny's worth of bon bons? My lady had a remarkable facility to adapt to the occasion; those who slid to a halt from carpeted limousines, all flutter and furs, for a quarter of Romance Assorted and the weekly cheroots, were greeted with a beautifully intonated: 'how are you ... and the care? All well?'

Minutes later the local dead-end kids, myself included, would make an appearance, and, in a decidedly different dialect, she would inform us that she had not got all day and our mothers should not give us so much to spend in the first place. In those faraway days, three pence was a fortune, a veritable blank cheque for twelve caramels, a lucky bag and a packet of sweet cigarettes.

That shop is engraved on my mind from the first day I found that I could, with a little help from my friends, see over the counter. I can still see the display boxes of chocolates and the pyramid of jaffas, strings of bananas from God knows where. On the wall were pinioned the huge cigarette displays for Craven A and sea-going John Player. The paper packet of five Woodbines would be enjoyed behind the wall nearby. I wonder too do the children of today still crack the penny bars into a thousand pieces, then the whole gang could benefit from their pal's good fortune.

That shop had a social significance for the area, it was a meeting place, a sort of cross-roads where the news of the day could be discussed and great events anticipated. From early morning to late into the night it was a cheerful beacon on what was then a very quiet road.

The shop is gone and the keeper too.

Shopping made easy [from the John Minihan collection]

THE GARDENER

Along the grey, mist-damp road his black leather, Sunday-best, shoes had for years, clapped his coming and passing by my bedroom window, minutes before the half-hour bell for first Mass trembled across the sleeping fields. Then, one Sunday morning, just the bells woke me and I knew my friend in the heavy black coat and cloth cap had walked out of this life and into my mind. He had toiled six days a week in the gardens of the rich and I had first met him one Monday morning as I waited for the bus to school. I remember how he answered every contentious or pessimistic view of life with the all-embracing comment: 'Sure we're only passing through'.

He was undeniably proud of his calling but I did see, at times, flashes of embarrassment cross his leathery countenance as his spade or fork dislodged itself and crashed down on an irate conductor's platform. It was always late evening before he trudged home to a loving wife and a hot meal.

His Sunday morning ritual was worthy of observation. He always sat in the same corner of the church, wrapped in personal prayer but not oblivious to the act of worship on the altar. His cap too had a special place on the high window ledge above his bowed head. After Mass it was time for a fatherly chat with the youngsters who joyfully crammed the blue Legion of Mary box, like puppets in a Punch and Judy show. The *Universe* under his arm he shunned 'those foreign papers' it was over to the little shop for his week's supply of plug. Home then to his cottage of open fire, stone-floor kitchen and his old Pye radio, which ran on those marvellous wet glass batteries. An odd Sunday afternoon it was 'down the Park to see the Rockies', devotions in the evening and then home to bed for the first-bus start to another week of grass cutting, hedge clipping, path brushing, back breaking.

Now he is gone and the world seems no poorer for his absence but I like to think there are those who miss his quiet, strong presence in an extrovert, shallow world.

In a class of his own

I'm not well at all, you know, and I blame the mid-term break. You know the symptoms; tired after a hard day at the pit-head, behind the counter, wherever the good Lord has deigned to slot us. You haul yourself to the nearest chair and summon all your strength to watch telly and a quiet evening by the fire. Then it begins.

'Dad, I need help with my lessons.' Through the haze I could see there were two of them.

'Ask your mother,' I suggested.

'She says that you were at school longer than she was and you are to do it,' they said. 'She says that it would be good for you as you have nothing else to do.'

'Ask her again,' I try, without much conviction. They toddle off.

Noise in kitchen, pots and pans do whatever pots and pans do when they are dropped on kitchen floor. Toddlers return.

'Dad, Mum says that you know more about these things than she does as she went to a different school.'

Somehow, in my collapsed state, I missed the subtlety of her point about different schools. In my time, boys played hurling or rugby and girls cheered on the sidelines, that was the only discernible difference in the sexes. I was to learn later that there were others.

Back to school. Things have changed for the worse since my time, 'ins na ranganna'. Time was when all you ever needed to know was that 2 + 2 = 4 and all problems were fairly straightforward. Now, someone ordains that our children are above such basic tests. Now it's a case of 2 + something = 4. Fiendishly clever stuff, find out the missing something. Higher maths was never good with me. Dad bites pencil, furrows brow, tries to look intelligent with one eye on the telly.

There is another child on the horizon as the first two puzzle to themselves why their Dad cannot do simple equations. Son number two has what looks like a car in his hand but I'm due for a rude awakening.

'Bet you Dad, you could not change this into a pre-historic monster', the word was bigger than himself but it tripped off the tongue. I was not to know the plastic toy was one of those transformers. Half an hour later I was no nearer a solution to the task set by the little ... lad! He looked at me with disappointment.

'It's OK Dad, I'll get my brother to fix it.' He joined the others and from the scraps of conversation that reached my ears they had decided that I was not the complete man they had considered me to be.

All this led me to ponder on the incredible role played by teachers each day of their working lives. I am full of unabashed admiration for their patience with the increasing number of children with whom they have to deal. I have stood in awe of the profession since my very early days and one man first sparked that faith.

For forty years he was a teacher of children, an unpaid counsellor to the whole community in which he lived. Teaching then bordered on the pioneer. He walked or biked to school along mud roads, stoked fire grates, dusted tables before pale-faced charges arrived, cold and wet in the yard outside. The equipment was basic. The local slate quarry provided the class with their first writing pads. The teacher then, and, in some areas still, was the educator, settler of feuds, righter of wrongs and unpaid psychiatrist.

He stood, in the eyes of the people, on the same pedestal as the local priest and one above the doctor. He had to cram a lifetime of education into six years for those who would know no other level, and, indeed, would need no other. He fitted them for jobs, applied for same and prayed at night for the wayward ones who needed only one spark of insight to release the locked up potential of a good citizen of a young state.

He was the cultural link with the past, preserving a fine heritage and inculcating a new generation with a respect for the language which was already losing the battle because the system was wrong, not its agents. Government departments and inspectors changed but teachers, God willing, were expected to go on.

Adjusting to change, he was a well-seasoned ash, bending, never breaking, springing back against pressure. Teacher organisations were to give voice, at last, to his grievances, such as they were. Retirement came and parents of children, now parents, all past-pupils, have never forgotten him. No more the squeak of chalk on board and slate, the school is gone but fond memories still warm like good brandy.

Day-off – pupils and teachers before boarding the train to Youghal for a day at the sea

ORCHARDS OF YOUTH

They've built houses in the orchard of my youth. There was an orchard which attracted as no other. It was surrounded by great, twenty-foot, natural stone walls but the ingenuity of our short-pants gang was incredible. A tree grew outside the walls and we would do wax a gaza and swing like chattering monkeys onto the top of the wall. There they would stand, their topmost branches level with the wall on which we sat with a collective eye for the possible approach of the farmer-owner and the other surveying the crimson bounty glistening in the sunshine.

From our lofty perch it was child's play to leap across to the nearest branch and 'Operation Apple' was in progress. It was amazing the number of apples that were stuffable into tiny pockets. It was a wonderful test of the tailors of the time, that seams seldom gave way under the weight and, when they did, there were wonderful people called mothers who would sew them up again.

Did they know the cause of the wear and tear? I think so, but they had the wisdom not to inquire too deeply as to the origin of the contents of the apple tart. Now fathers were different; they were not to be trusted with such classified information. They had the unfortunate habit of asking straight questions and insisting on straight answers. Fathers could be ungrateful creatures.

There was never a problem slocking that particular orchard until the farmer had a brainwave. He decided to keep his favourite bull there. We thought he was introduced as something of a watch-dog; innocence is a marvellous gift and we were not to know that it was the first breeding station in the area. That farmer was ahead of his time.

It did pose a problem. We were fine in the safety of the branches but one slip and we would have to make like El Cordobes with our shirts. He was to become one of the most confused bulls of all time. Our plan would be to attack from both sides, distracting our four-legged friend in the process. There was a boy, now a man, who still bears the scar of one encounter. A branch broke and, before he got back up the tree, our bull had left his mark. The pants was beyond repair. We were all sworn to secrecy on that sunlit day many years ago.

There was another orchard where 'The Secret Garden' might have been set. It had an eerie feel to it; great smooth walls covered in lichen, ivy and moss, brambles wrapped round old gooseberry bushes, underneath apple and plum trees, gnarled, leafless and spent. It could be reached through an old, red-tiled pantry and shadowy passageway, on to an arched gateway. The old paths were overgrown and there were thorn scratches for those who dared to explore. I was in my element.

It possessed all the possibilities of adventure which the fertile mind could muster on evenings when the sunshine filtered through cracks in the west wall.

I did not live there but came to visit and there was a neighbour's child. We never even held hands but talked for hours, on a broken garden seat, of a world about which we knew little. It was, I suppose, first love and Buddy Holly had yet to rain in our hearts.

Tour de Cork – Father-in-law the late Gilbert O'Connell and his pal Bran cross Patrick's Bridge

Memories of some last picture shows

My father was a creature of habit, a sense of discipline which stood him in good stead over the years. On one evening each week he would after work meet my mother outside the Pav. There would be high tea in the restaurant and then into the cinema for the latest film. My mother's favourite was Walter Pidgeon but I never did find out which starlet my dad fancied, but I'd guess it would have been a young Bette Davis.

I wonder how many sons and daughters would have similar memories and how many generations of parents enjoyed similar breaks from the routine of living in the 1940s, 1950s and early 1960s.

It would be the 1960s before television would have nation-wide impact, so in a real social sense, going to the pictures had a special place. In its time it had replaced platform dancing at the cross-roads, the fit-up theatre in the market field, and earlier the simple chat at the village pump, for thousands who would come to work and live in the cities.

Although going to the flicks was passive in a sense, it did not have the awful stultifying effect of the television. There was the dressing up, the getting there by bus, or the rushing out from the workplace at six to catch the full programme which was generous by today's standards.

If my memory is correct, at the Savoy, Cork there would have been a newsreel, a second feature, a sing-along with the theatre organist, complete with words on a rolled screen, a trailer and the feature. Is it any wonder that tickets for Sunday nights were like a seat on the bench with Jack Charlton in Cagliari. I remember clearly the brisk trade outside the Savoy and tickets would exchange hands at more than double their original market value.

Each cinema too had its own character. The Palace, which is looking like a youngster again as the Everyman Palace, had a particular buzz and for some reason I remember it best for its short funnies. The Ritz had those

Meet me at the Pav

smashing double seats which brought you that much nearer to the one you loved at the time. If you were on the lang from school for the afternoon, the Lee had a quiet, discreet charm.

The Capitol, the great survivor and doing good business as a cineplex, was always considered the baby of the Cork cinema family and I'll remember to my dying day, falling in love with Shirley Jones in *Carousel*. The big wide screen and the then advanced sound system made it the wonder of that innocent age. I could almost taste the clams and felt I knew Gordon McCrea personally as he walked the beach and sang about the birth of his son, or was it his daughter? Actually it was both, as Gordon realised that his heir might turn out to be his heiress.

Is there anyone out there who considers such film trivia important. I know I do. Cinema was an educator in the broadest and best sense and I've never met a boring film buff.

Of course there were what we might describe as the fringe theatres and I'm bound to leave out one or two, but I can recall the Imperial in Oliver Plunkett Street. Who could ever forget the Assembly Rooms on the Mall, now enjoying a new lease of life as a restaurant? And there was the northside's pride and joy, The Lido. The Coliseum (The Col to all) had a corner all to itself and is now the venue for leisure for another generation of Corkonians. Much later, another popular venue would be the Cameo on Military Road.

Wherever you live, no matter what village town or city, the picture house will hold a particular attraction for you. It seems such a long time since the days of travelling cinema with the sheet hung on the community hall wall and the hard bench seats. Ah, the sheer excitement when the lights would go out, and there before your very eyes would be the flickering image of Gene Autry or Roy Rogers, or my favourite, the Cisco Kid, thundering to the rescue of the girl in calico with the faraway whimsical look.

I think we lost something, somewhere.

Rationing and gas masks

After the Second World War the world had to do without and Ireland was no exception. Rationing cards still lay in sideboard drawers; gas masks looked threateningly down from the tops of wardrobes. I can remember big Jaffa oranges being a rare treat. I'm not sure of the years but pocket money on a Sunday would be two old pence and you were flying if you were given an English three penny bit. A shilling was out of the question and a half-crown was wealth and seen only on Communion and Confirmation days.

Anyway, back to cinema days. As I grew older, I would spend the whole week scheming, planning and getting inside Dad and around Mum to let me go to the flicks on the Saturday. I would brush the yard, my teeth, do my homework, wash up, even go to bed early, anything, just to get permission to see the latest on the silver screen. It would have been no more than the latest western or war film. I'm unable to watch them now without thinking that they did really glorify death.

Then Randolph Scott, Alan Ladd, John Wayne or Gary Cooper could do no wrong and the Red Indians were always the bad guys who rode bareback and bit the dust as your man, the hero, would blow the smoke from the gun and smile at the heroine.

Some of the houses would run serials so they would be our *Glenroes* and *Fair City*s and we'd wait all week to see if your man really did die, or, would he rise again and shoot your man from the rooftop. He always did, live that is, and invariably the 'boyo' on the roof would be riddled and come tumbling down, hitting the wooden lean-to on the way which, of course, broke his fall, but we were not to know that.

Sometimes, we'd miss a week and would spend the first five minutes of the next episode asking those around us what had happened, much to the annoyance of the adults.

I've always been an old romantic and I must have fallen in love with every leading lady in every musical that ever reached the screen. I'll never forget the updating of *Carmen* with Dorothy Dandridge and Harry Belafonte in *Carmen Jones* and *The King and I* with Yul Brynner and Deborah Kerr. By the time the 1960s came along the boy had become a man and the late Audrey Hepburn had stolen my heart in *My Fair Lady* as she had done in *Roman Holiday.*

People go to the cinema as they have done for generations to be with each other and share a comedy, a blast from the past, or, the more real modern product where little is left to the imagination. The musical and western have seen their glory days and it takes a Clint Eastwood to set the six shooters smokin' again, but more likely he'll have turned cop or detective. And the wagon wheel has turned. History has been re-written. The Indians have Daniel Day Lewis as the *Last of the Mohicans* and the bush-whacking, bounty-hunting cowboys have been shown in a more real light.

My earliest memory of going to the pictures remains like a still of an old black and white classic imprinted on the mind. In fact, it was not the first film I had seen. I was brought, as a Christmas treat, to the cartoon shows in the former Munster Arcade, or, was it Cashs? No, it was definitely the Arcade. Anyway, you got your present from Santa and the ticket entitled you to a free film show.

I still think Donald Duck is wonderful, even if I have never understood a word he has said. There was another guy, Elmer Fudd, now he has never been bettered with the exceptions of Bugs Bunny, and, more recently, The Road Runner. But I digress.

The occasion to which I refer was a much more adult adventure. I was allowed, for the first time, to tag along with an older brother to a Wednesday afternoon showing at the Savoy. Now, I have never been to paradise and there must be some doubt as to whether I will ever reach such lofty heights, but, I've been to 'The Gods'.

The route, as life itself, was very much an uphill battle as once your ticket was secured at one of the kiosks on either side of the main foyer, you went back out into Patrick Street, ticket in hot hand, and down the narrow street where the open door led to a flight of stone steps.

When you are young, everything seems huge and going on forever which is just the way it was then. We ran up those flights with an almighty clatter and when we reached the top we got a ticking off for all the noise. I thought we'd been sent back to the street, but we were allowed through the door. And there we were, on top of the world, our world. That magnificent picture house lay before us and the big screen seemed miles away. I was in my element.

On the way home from the flicks I'd be Humphrey Bogart, Jimmy Stewart, and, I'd be falling in love with Lauren Bacall, or much later, the girl of my late-teen dreams, Grace Kelly. My hot breath would fog up the bus window. I'd trace their names on the window, romantic fool that I was and, God knows, remain.

But romance was the key to it all. When we went to the pictures then, we had hardly been outside the parish, so, as the stage-coach came hurtling into town with the guard already shot to pieces by the baddie, we were off to another world, the badlands. And talking of heroes, when Gary Cooper tipped his hat and waited for his *High Noon,* sure we were there to a man with him. No one was going to take over 'this here town while myself and Yep were around ... doggone.'

MAKE 'EM LAUGH

Laughter, you might say, is the essential ingredient in the pudding-bowl mix of life. The ability to see the funny side of things, or even of oneself, must rank up there with regular exercise and good diet in the pecking order for survival. Laughter is a very personal affair. That which will leave some tickled pink may leave others unmoved and stony-faced.

The art of the true laughter-maker is heaven-sent, elusive, and in every generation, bestowed only on the few.

Jack Benny did nothing and people collapsed with laughter; crossing over the invisible divide between the viewer at home and the studio space removed in distance and time.

Woody Allen held Diane Keaton in a romantic embrace, looked in a mirror and spoke to himself about how meaningless life was in the Big Apple. He lost the girl but won the audience. He was being the all-time put-upon, unsure guy, and we could identify with that.

W. C. Fields, on screen, debunked all we still hold dear, could not stand children and would not work with animals. He had a put-down for all he came in contact with and we hated him for it, but still rolled in the cinema aisles years ago. Some of us rush home now to see a re-run of the man on feature-revival on telly.

Bob Hope has a one-liner for every occasion. He still hones rapid-fire quips, the work of a team of script-writers. Delivery is all when it's a Hope or Groucho Marx riposte.

We had and have our funny men too. Sure we are bound to have, as there is the comic in all of us, but some are gifted, and the Irish can spot them a mile off.

Jimmy O'Dea was one of the blessed; one of the chosen ones whose life's work was to put people in a better mood. As with all the greats, his was a concealed talent; it looked easy but being funny never is, it is the brittle

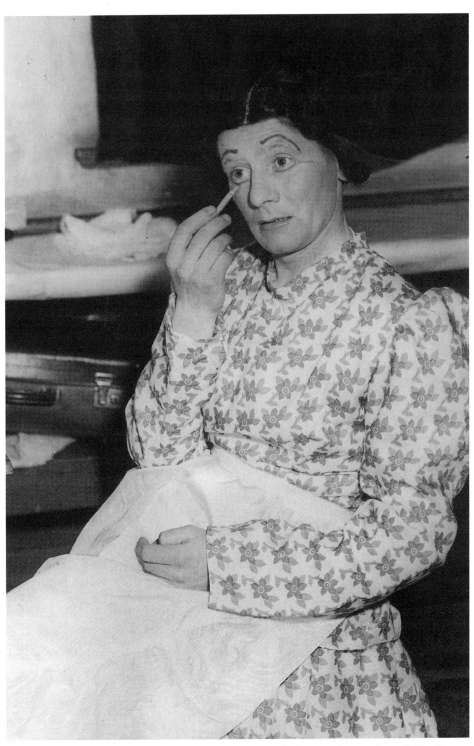

On with the motley – great panto dame Ignatius Comerford puts on the powder and the paint

edge of the public performance.

Nowadays, Niall Tobin's ear for accents, and his ability to hold that mirror up to life in modern Ireland, fills theatres and gets us out of ourselves.

Up there with the best, I would put Ignatius Comerford. Illness meant Ignatius left the stage some forty-three years ago at the height of his considerable powers. For those who never saw him perform, there can be no measure of their loss; for those of us who looked up wide-eyed to him on stage, here was the definitive Dame, the bright spark of post-Christmas childhood days and nights.

As I reminisced about Ignatius on a cold night, sleet-laden wind swirled around and the sky was a sombre black, but I could feel a lightness. I had been lucky enough to have a faded but nonetheless important childhood memory of his walking across the old Opera House stage. He was the Dame and panto is all about traditional values – as it is today with the likes of Billa O'Connell and Paddy Comerford.

A fairy-tale castle, pumpkin coach, stuff of theatrical dreams which make life's realities more bearable. Ignatius Comerford brought that essential colour and magic to all who ever saw him on stage. That is sufficient achievement in any one life.

All dolled up! Paddy Comerford and Billa O'Connell

IMPULSE VISIT

I found myself ... only an hour from Dublin. I was driving down from Cavan, through Navan, and, south along the new bridge over the Boyne. Down the road lies Dalgan Park, home to the Columban Fathers. In what seems another life now, in the late 1950s and early 1960s, I had spent over four years there as a student. Finding that vocationally I did not have the necessary staying power, I left to lead the life I have led since.

There have been no regrets and though I had never actually gone back to Dalgan in all those years, I had never lost the grá for the place and I always savoured the fine memories which it held for me.

You could say, I suppose, that it made a man of me, though those that know me now might dispute even that.

On an impulse, that crisp morning, I decided to swing off the road, drive between the tree cover, and there it stood, the imposing Dalgan building, the cut stone reflecting the low-flying, intermittent sun, just as I had left it over thirty years ago.

Have you ever noticed how, when you return to a place which has meant something to you, that you get that little shiver up the spine and the mouth goes a little dry?

Dalgan, the building, has not changed at all. The rich wooden floored corridors leading to the twin doors of the seminary chapel are still spotless and shining with that comforting smell of polish. The display rooms, off the corridors, reflect the work of the missionaries from those first travels to the Far East when Corkman Bishop Edward Galvin moved with such courage in unknown territory. He and his colleagues brought the Faith to the Chinese, hence the order's founding title 'The Maynooth Mission to China'.

In another room lie the chalice and other effects of the late Father John Blowick, revered to this day in his native Mayo and wherever his wonderful influence was felt. I knew Father John. He had a kind word for everyone and always encouraged, especially when the word of praise was just what was needed by a struggling student.

Outside, the rolling landmass of Meath moves south to Tara's Hill. In Dalgan's grounds the path, round the GAA cum soccer pitch, leads to a sheltered corner, away from the busy road to Dublin beyond the trees.

There lies the neatly kept graveyard with the roll of honour chiselled on the grey monument running the length of ordered headstones set in grass. There the men who went to their reward rest in Dalgan, and the names on the grey wall represent too those who lay down in foreign fields, their work completed.

I am not a great visitor of graveyards but there was a real sense of peace just standing there, spotting names whom I knew as dedicated people following their light and trying to shed some for those with whom they came in contact. Life is never perfect but there are those who help make the jigsaw pieces fit more easily for others. That's the odd thing too, we have no idea how our little actions can affect those who come within our influence. The men and women, who now have left this world, still exercise that influence for good. It makes you think.

But life is about living and the Columbans continue to work all over the world wherever they are made welcome and wherever there is need for their work. I have always thought that leaving home, loved ones and country, to follow your spiritual star takes a special kind of courage. How tough it must have been for those missionaries when travel was a question of weeks not days nor hours, and when trips back home were few and far between. I've been told there are those who become so absorbed in their work, those who become so much part of the culture and society in which they move, that they just wish for the strength to carry on their work in faraway places with strange sounding names.

As I say, I have never regretted the going to or the leaving of Dalgan. It was a chapter in my life. Looking back now my return to civilian life must have been a real disappointment to my father. My mother said, even before

I went there, that I'd never survive without the company of girls. She was right. Dad never once made me feel that I had in some way left him down, dashed his hopes of having a priest in the family. His only concern was that I would be happy in whatever I did. He met me at the station platform. It was good to be home.

A stroll near Royal Tara's Hill

THE INCREDIBLE JOURNEY

Mary lay next to her sleeping husband, listening to that eerie silence of a house draped in a fall of snow. Tom always slept deep – that rest of the just, in fact. But there would be no peace of mind that night for troubled Mary. The year was 1850.

The snow outside threw a white glow through the thatched cottage and her eyes had, hours before, become accustomed to the dark.

Near the bed a rag doll lay on the dresser with her head in her chest, half propped against the rough wall. It belonged to Nan, Mary's eldest child and only daughter. Nan lived with her forester husband 20 miles away. They had five children in nine years of marriage and her sixth was due any day.

Now Mary had a gift. It was not so much that she could see things which had yet to happen, but rather that she lived the joys and sorrows of those near to her as they themselves experienced them. For days she fretted about her daughter's welfare and this night she was overwhelmed with the feeling that her child was dying.

Her decision, like the snow, came quickly that November night. She got up without waking her husband and dressed herself by the light of the candle, wrapping against the cold with her flowing black cloak.

Without as much as leaving a sign to Tom as to her movements, she set out in the ankle-deep snow which was turning to slush as the dawn filtered from the east.

She began her incredible, 20-mile journey of courage. Out of the valley she climbed through the drifts of melting ice pools, along mud roads, tracked furrow-deep by dray, cart and trap wheels. The early light flickered and died as snow-laden clouds rolled up from the south-east. Only a mother's courage and love kept her going.

Then she heard it – almost imperceptible at first but soon there was no mistaking the squelch and thud of wheels on the rough road, stretching like some great black ribbon on virginal white. When the dray drew level her tears of relief mingled with those caused by the biting, grey cold. She knew the man at the reins as an old friend of her own father – Nan's grandfather.

She sat up and the strange pair rattled down the valley across the river to the south bank and they hit the town, hours later, in a blinding storm. They parted, and Mary travelled the last few weary miles alone and bone weary but driven on with that uncanny awareness of her loved one's need for her strong presence.

She reached the house, and was met by a scene which repeated on the theatre boards of the world to this day, would be dismissed as 'staged' – but this was very much real life stuff. The unfortunate woman in labour turned and tossed on the creaking bed; her distracted husband cradled their youngest, who had been woken by her mother's screams, 'the handy woman' of the time, rocked on a chair in a corner, muttering in a drunken stupor, no help to the pitiful woman on the bed who needed her skills.

All the weariness left Mary as she rushed to her daughter's side. She knew that there was little time to spare. Clearing the room she began to lead mother and unborn child back from death.

Years later the baby girl, born that night, married and, over the first child born to her, the gospel of St John was recited at baptism. The priest said it was to rid the infant of the demoniacal 'second sight' but truth to tell that child grew up with the 'gift' of seeing into the future, and it can be found in the family to this day.

No need to panic

It would appear that the old ways and customs come readily to mind around Christmas. I sense too that it is something of a welcome distraction from the somewhat unnerving thought that we are moving towards another New Year and all that it entails.

However, lie back and relax, ring down for Jeeves and order a lightly boiled egg and toast, give the old pillows another fluffing up – then we'll talk about the time that's in it.

Comfortable? Good, well the first thing not to do is to panic. I know you may know someone who has the Christmas presents wrapped since September and the turkey ordered since October, but not to worry, there are still about ... shopping days to Christmas. If you are not killed in the stampede, there is still time to catch up and gather up a zillion handkerchiefs, re-wrap some of the same you received last year, making sure they are not returned to sender, of course.

Now, as you sip that cuppa and tap on the egg, repeat to yourself ... 'I will not panic ... I will not panic ...' take three deep breaths, check that gift-list again and eat the egg before it goes cold.

There is a special buzz about the time leading up to Christmas and it does you no harm at all being caught up in the whole thing as long as you keep your priorities ... not much use getting het up about Christmas if you are flat on your back for the holidays from sheer exhaustion.

It is easy to say that Christmas long ago was a much less frenetic affair and there is no doubt that it was too. I think our expectations were not as high and we made do with less.

Santa certainly did not have to deal with the mega demands which are made on him these days, but sometimes we contribute to the hype ourselves and wonder why we are like wet rags on the day, too jaded to enjoy our free time with family and good friends.

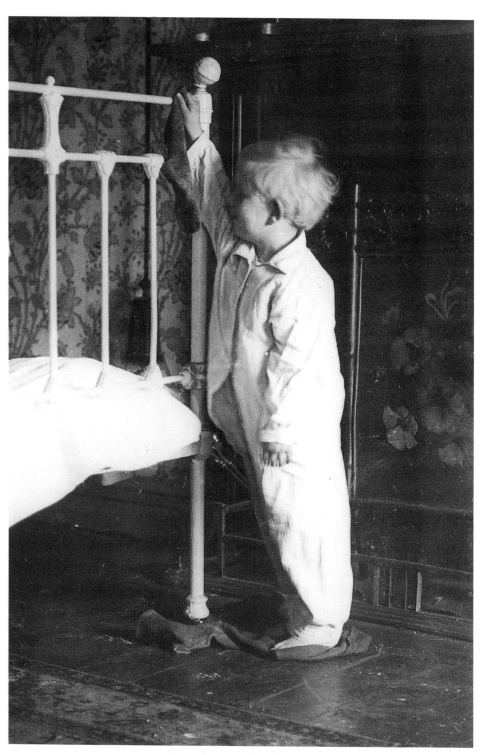

It was the night before Christmas

How many can recall that whole families did not stir outside the door on Christmas Day, except for early Mass or Church Service? It was very much a day in the home with a comforting kind of ritual observed by young and old. Generally, it was a very private day when parents and children stayed indoors and shared.

Not that it would be unknown for the blessed peace to be shattered by a flare-up between younger members. Mother would sense that the day was about to go rapidly downhill and step in with diplomatic skill which would not be out of place at the UN.

Then there is St Stephen's Day the peace of which would be shattered by a 'knock on the knocker and the ring at the bell and someone seeking a copper for ... singing so well'. Those were the days of the Wren Boys which, in recent years, have all but disappeared and more is the pity. Their demise relates directly to the loss of that tangible sense of community and even of the rural tradition. Their disappearance will not upset the balance of payments, reduce the interest rates nor apparently, affect our lives in any way, but, they were part of what we were and those little differences contributed to an identity which is continually eroded by our fixation with uniformity and fear of being ... different.

ANOTHER CHRISTMAS DAY

There was no light, darkness visible. I can still feel the weight of the shapes at the end of the bed; Santa had come, joy to the world. Noises from other rooms confirmed the rest; he had been and gone; the glass was empty, cake crumbs dotted the place ... he must have been starved.

Then the stampede to our parents' room and, their surprise, delight as the parcels were ripped open to reveal Meccano, soldier and farm sets for the boys. Our sister and older brothers had reached the age when the hop at the Boat Club on Stephen's Night occupied their minds but there would be no sleep in the house. Father was already marshalling the forces for Mass together. Sister got a new coat and the brothers, shirts... how Santa knew all the sizes was beyond the brother and myself.

We braved the cold wind outside, walking to Mass between Mum and Dad; she in her new fur coat with a new soft hat. There was always a stop and chat with my man in the coat and cap; old friends were best.

We thought that Mass would never end; there was so much to be done and only the whole day to do it. The visit to the crib was always special; strange how the animals look so much smaller now. I always thought it was mean not to put the three wise men in straight away. We could see them standing behind the crib and we considered it very rude that they were not asked in.

Mother worked in the tiny kitchen the whole morning and I never heard her complain even when the windows became steamed up or when the peas from the packet with the soda powder, spilled over the hot-plate.

We always had our aunt and uncle, on Mother's side, for Christmas dinner. She was a real lady and he was our joy as he would have been to the 'Club' and would be 'nicely' with the Christmas spirit. His rendering of 'Trumpeter, What Are You Sounding Now' seems to ring round the old house every Christmas Day.

The dinner went on for hours but, the cute ones, the brother and myself kept room for the plum pudding. When no one was looking, we'd light our portions from the remains of the whiskey and wonder later why we felt so sleepy. We put it down to the big blazing fire.

Curiously, I do not have a great memory of Christmas nights then; we may have been hustled off to bed early as the adults would have wilted after the sixth game of ludo and the world series in snakes and ladders.

The principal players have gone. Brothers and sister now make their own of Christmas Day; life's rich pattern unfolds for the children of another generation.

The old photos are back in the cardboard box – perhaps to be taken out at another time.

GLOSSARY

Arc: Arcadia Ballroom in Cork

Ar ealú ón scoil: on the lang from school: away from class without permission

Assembs: Assembly Rooms

'Bags': verb to claim

Barracka: Barrack Street in Cork

Bees' Knees: Wonderful

Blackas: Blackberries

Bumpers: Dodgem Rides

Clash of the ash: hurling match

Clipper Carlton and Dixies: Showbands

Crosser: Crosshaven

Dolling Ourselves Up: Getting ready to go to the dance

Dressed to the Nines: Well dressed

Dyke: Mardyke, picturesque area of Cork City

Eckers: School home-work

Flasked: Band of tin used to prevent hurley from splitting

Flicks: Cinema

Franciscan Sandals: Open leather scandals with straps

Grinds: Extra curricular help from expert prior to examination

Het Up: Upset

Holiers: Holidays

Jouram: Drink, pint of beer or Irish stout

Knuckles and gobs: Game played with white stones being tossed in the air and caught on the back of the hand

Majorca: Ballroom in Crosshaven, County Cork

Melodious: Wonderful

Merries: Carnival, Fun Fair

Pana: Patrick Street in Cork City

Pitch and Toss: Game played with coin and stone marker

Pontoon: Card game

Redbarn: Ballroom in Youghal, County Cork

Release: A game of chasing, catching and earning release of team members by racing into defined area

Shandona: Shandon Street in Cork

Slocking: Stealing Apples

Tawneens (Thorneens): Minute silver scaled fish

Tennis Hops: Dances

The Pav: Pavilion Cinema

Tog Off: Undress

Wax a gaza: Climb a gas lamp

Woolies: Department store

Yanks: Upper Cork Harbour area of Lough Mahon, on the Blackrock Peninsula

ACKNOWLEDGEMENTS

My special thanks are due to the Board of *The Examiner* Publications and in particular to Secretary/Director Anthony Dinan for generous access to *The Examiner* archives and to the work of its photographers, past and present. I am particularly grateful to Lillian Caverley for all her research. I acknowledge also the use of text first published in *The Examiner*.

I acknowledge the use of photographic material: John Minihan's shop study, p. 115, the author's picture on the cover; a picture by M. J. Doolan, p. 81; and from G. and V. Healy, Noel Hickey; Frank Fitzgerald; Paddy Clarke and RTE. Every effort has been made to establish sources of all photographs used and acknowledgement given – should a source have not been acknowledged, I take this opportunity of apologising for such an oversight and will make the necessary correction at the first opportunity.

I would like to acknowledge the support I received from my *Examiner* colleagues – particularly Tina Neylon, Literary Editor; GAA writer Jim O'Sullivan and Rugby writer Barry Coughlan for their invaluable help. A special word of thanks to Anne Healy in the preparation of this book.